SADLIER
FAITH AND
WITNESS

CHURCH HISTORY

A Course on
the People of God

Rev. Thomas J. Shelley, Ph.D.

William H. Sadlier, Inc.
9 Pine Street
New York, New York 10005-1002

Acknowledgments

Scripture selections are taken from the *New American Bible* Copyright © 1991, 1986, 1970 by the Confraternity of Christian Doctrine, Washington, D.C. and are used with permission. All rights reserved.

Excerpts from the English translation of *The Roman Missal* © 1973, International Committee on English in the Liturgy, Inc. (ICEL); English translation of the Prayer of Christian Unity from *The Roman Missal* © 1973, ICEL; an excerpt from the *Rite of Penance* © 1974, ICEL; excerpts from the English translation of *Holy Communion and the Worship of the Eucharist outside Mass* © 1974, ICEL. All rights reserved.

Excerpts from *The Documents of Vatican II*, Walter M. Abbott, S. J. General Editor, © 1966 by America Press, Inc.

Excerpt from the Ancient Arapaho Invocation, St. Stephen's Indian Mission, Wind River Reservation.

English translation of the "Gloria Patri" by the International Consultation on English Texts (ICET). All rights reserved.

Excerpt from the preface to *The Nigger of the Narcissus*, Joseph Conrad, 1898.

"Joyful, Joyful We Adore Thee," reprinted with the permission of Scribner, a Division of Simon & Schuster from *The Poems of Henry Van Dyke*. Copyright 1911 by Charles Scribner's Son, renewed 1939 by Teritus Van Dyke.

Excerpts from *Catholic Household Blessings and Prayers* © 1988, United States Catholic Conference, Washington, D.C. are used by permission of the copyright owner. All rights reserved.

Excerpt from *Praying with Hildegard of Bingen* (Durka) (Winona, MN: Saint Mary's Press, 1991). Used by permission of the publisher. All rights reserved.

Excerpt from *Praying with Julian* (Durka) (Winona, MN: Saint Mary's Press, 1989). Used by permission of the publisher. All rights reserved.

"The Canticle of Brother Sun" was adapted by Ken Ford and Richard Duprey for the musical *Francis*, originally produced and directed by Frank A. Martin. Found in *The Francis Book: 800 Years with the Saint from Assisi* compiled by Roy Gasnick, O.F.M. Macmillan Publishing, Co. Inc., New York, 1980.

Excerpt of the "Memorare," Saint Bernard from *The Treasury of the Holy Spirit*, compiled by Msgr. Michael Buckley and published by Hodder and Stroughton, London, England.

"A Lenten Prayer," Saint Gregory the Great, translated by Peter J. Scagnelli. Used with permission.

"Prayer of Praise," words by Saint Thomas Aquinas, © Geoffery Chapman (an imprint of Cassell plc) London, England.

Cover Illustrator: Wendy Grossman
Map Illustrator: Mapping Specialists, Ltd.

Cover Photos

Art Resource, NY: front, top background. *Catholic News Service*/ Michael Edrington: front, bottom left. *Crosiers*/Gene Plaisted, OSC: front, center. *Gamma Liaison Network*/ Livio Anticoli: back, bottom. *Granger Collection:* back, top. *Ramon José Lopez:* back, center.

Photo Credits

Jim Saylor   Lori Berkowitz
Photo Editor   *Associate Photo Editor*

Adventure Photo & Film/ Uli Wiesmeir: 18–19; Colin Monteath: 66–67. *Diane J. Ali:* 12–13, 142 right. *The Archdiocese of Chicago*/ Jean Clough: 189. *Archive Photos:* 86, 164, 165 top, 166 right; David Ake: 44; Blake Sell: 114–115. *Art Resource, NY:* 15 top, 38, 48 center, 48 right, 50, 56, 59, 60 bottom, 61, 72, 118, 120–121, 123, 131, 177 left, 181 right; Erich Lessing: 10 right, 13 left, 84, 176; Scala: 35 top, 73, 80, 87, 180 right and center, 181 left; A.M. Rosati: 37; Giraudon: 92, 97, 178; Victoria and Albert Museum: 98; Pierpont Morgan Library: 82 right; Scibilia: 180 left; Gian Berto Vanni: 178 right. *Bettman:* 14 bottom center, 32 right, 147, 155 top, 166 left. *Lori Berkowitz:* 108 left, 109 background, 144 top. *Myrleen Cate:* 14 bottom left. *Bill Coleman:* 83. *Catholic News Service:* 14 top left, 14 top right, 14 bottom right, 96 left, 155 bottom, 157 top, 157 bottom, 159, 165 bottom; Joanne Keane: 15 bottom; Joe Rimkus, Jr.: 170–171; Michael Edrington: 171. *Dwight Cendrowski:* 168. *Christie's Images:* 24. *Corbis*/ Bartolome Estaban Murillo, National Gallery of London: 10 left; Owen Franken: 32 left; Hubert Stadler: 35 bottom; Angelo Hornack: 63. *Crosiers*/ Gene Plaisted, OSC: 48 left, 49, 96 center, 135, 140, 186. *E.T. Archives:* 132. *FPG*/ Gary Buss: 70–71; LPI'84: 128; Arthur Tilley: 150. The Franciscans: 133 both. *Gamma Liaison Network*/ Arvino Garg: 10 center; Kathleen Campbell: 10–11. *Granger Collection:* 13 right, 34, 36, 60 top, 81, 82 left, 94 left, 94 right, 96 right, 99, 108 right, 109 top, 122, 142 left, 146, 152, 153, 154, 158, 182 left, 187.

Arthur Hastings: 38–39. *Image Bank*/ Michel Tcherevkoff: 11 right; Will Crocker: 27; Grant V. Faint: 74; Steve Bronstien: 90–91; David Gould: 98–99; G & V Chapman: 104; Mike Quon: 105; Michael Schneps: 106–107; John Lewis Stage: 107; Hans Neleman: 110–111; Blue Lemon Productions: 118–119; Elle Schuster: 126–127; Joseph McNally: 150–151; Steven Hunt: 162–163. *Image Works*/ Francisco Rangel: 183. *International Stock*/ Andre Hote: 62. *Greg Lord:* 119, 182 right. *Maryknoll:* 156, 167. *NASA:* 111. *National Geographic:* 78–79; Robert W. Madden: 46. *N.Y. Public Library:* 144 bottom, 145 top. *Office Central de Lisieux:* 188. *Photonica*/ Harriet Zucker: 8–9; Reider & Walsh: 25. *Pictorial History Research:* 134. *H. Armstrong Roberts:* 179. *St. Joseph's Abbey*/ Br. Emmanuel Morinelli, OCSO: 47. *Chris Sheridan:* 75. *Sisters of Charity of St. Elizabeth:* 145 bottom. *Sisters of Mercy:* 130. *Sportschrome*/ Robert Tringali: 128–129. *Stock Imagery*/ Fotopic: 86–87. *Stock Market:* 177 right. *Superstock:* 6. *Sygma:* 169; G. Giansanti: 11 left, 68–69, 95, 174–175. *Tony Stone Images:* 6–7, 48 background, 51; John Elk: 30–31; Robert Freck: 33, 58–59; Chris Noble: 42–43; Joe Cornish: 54–55; Randy Wells: 56–57; Claire Hayden: 80–81; Doug Armand: 92–93; Chris Johns: 116–117; David Hiser: 138–139; Liz Hymans: 142–143; Alan Abramowitz: 185. *Ursuline Academy:* 143. *U.S. Holocaust Memorial Museum:* 164–165. *Westlight:* 20–21.*Westock*/ Bryan Peterson: 102–103.

General Consultant
Rev. Joseph A. Komonchak, Ph.D.

Official Theological Consultant
Most Rev. Edward K. Braxton, Ph.D., S.T.D.
Auxiliary Bishop of St. Louis

Publisher
Gerard F. Baumbach, Ed.D.

Editor in Chief
Moya Gullage

Pastoral Consultant
Rev. Msgr. John F. Barry

Scriptural Consultant
Rev. Donald Senior, C.P., Ph.D., S.T.D.

General Editors
Norman F. Josaitis, S.T.D.
Rev. Michael J. Lanning, O.F.M.

Catechetical and Liturgical Consultants
Eleanor Ann Brownell, D. Min.
Joseph F. Sweeney
Helen Hemmer, I.H.M.
Mary Frances Hession
Maureen Sullivan, O.P., Ph.D.
Don Boyd

"The Ad Hoc Committee to Oversee the Use of the Catechism,
National Conference of Catholic Bishops,
has found this catechetical text to be in conformity
with the *Catechism of the Catholic Church*."

Home Office:
9 Pine Street
New York, NY 10005–1002

ISBN: 8215-5605-3
11 12/05

CHAPTER 1

EVER ANCIENT AND EVER NEW

Behold, I am with you always,
until the end of the age.

Matthew 28:20

"To be ignorant of what occurred before you were born is always to remain a child."
Cicero (106–43 B.C.)

What does this statement mean to you? Do you agree or disagree with it? Why?

Signs of Maturity

When we reach a certain age, our parents and teachers no longer call us children. Instead they begin to speak of us as adolescents or teenagers. This is a change that we welcome, for at this stage in our lives, we like to think that we are well on the way to becoming adults. By this time we have lost interest in the things that pleased us as children. This is all a natural part of growing up and achieving maturity.

One sign of maturity is that we no longer think only of the present moment. We begin to look forward to the future, to think about the rest of our education, and even to consider what kind of job or career we would like to have after we finish that education.

Another sign of maturity is that we begin to reflect on the past, to think about our roots—our family background, our heritage as Americans, and our religious traditions. This active reflection about the past is called the study of *history*.

Why History

Reread the statement by the ancient Roman author Cicero at the beginning of this lesson. Cicero seems to be saying that a child lives only for the present moment. An adult, on the other hand, looks to the past to make sense of the present. That is the most practical value of the study of history.

Another reason for studying history is well expressed in the comment of American poet Wallace Stevens that "all history is modern history." What Stevens is saying is that in a very important way, we are the sum total of all that has gone before us. By studying history, therefore, we learn something not only about the past but also about ourselves and our identities.

As Americans we are part of a nation that goes back over two hundred years. As Catholics we are part of an even bigger and older community, a Church that goes back ten times as far in time as our American republic. A Catholic writer once said that one of the most wonderful things about being a

Catholic is that it preserves us from the terrible fate of simply being children of our own age.

There is, however, another special reason why Catholics are interested in history: Our faith is rooted in actual historical events. Let's look at an example. Have you ever noticed that when we recite the creed at Mass on Sunday, we mention five names: God the Father, God the Son, God the Holy Spirit, the Blessed Virgin Mary, and—of all people—the Roman procurator Pontius Pilate?

Why mention Pilate? The answer is simple: It is not to honor Pilate but to remind us that at a particular time and place in human history, God became Man, suffered "under Pontius Pilate," died, and rose from the dead.

In this way the creed states the very opposite of what a story implies when it begins with the phrase "once upon a time." Whenever a story begins that way, we immediately know that what follows it is fiction, not fact. In mentioning Pilate,

on the other hand, the creed proclaims one of a series of historical facts that has had serious consequences for humanity. Knowing as much as we can about our Catholic history, therefore, helps us understand our faith more deeply and see it rooted in real facts—not fiction!

Yet one more benefit we can obtain from studying history is implied in the statement that "those who cannot remember the past are condemned to repeat it." As human beings we have the ability to learn. Those who have no knowledge of the past, however, cannot learn so easily. They are likely to repeat the mistakes of the past because they are unaware that others have already made them. Similarly, knowing about past successes helps us because those successes provide us with "working blueprints" for achievement.

 Can you think of any other reasons to study history? What are they?

9

People—and More

You have probably noticed that the word *history* contains the word *story*. That is because history is basically the story of the past. Of what, then, is that story made up? It is made up of people, places, buildings, events, and ideas.

People   The American writer Ralph Waldo Emerson once said that "there is properly no history, only biography." What Emerson meant is that history is made by people. There would be no history without people. This is certainly true of Church history. Its pages are filled with the stories of all kinds of remarkable men and women. From the early martyrs through the medieval monks down to the outstanding figures of our own day, the drama of Church history presents us with a truly colorful cast of human characters.

It would be a great mistake, however, to think that Church history is just the story of holy or perfect people. On the contrary, the Church is a Church of sinners as well as saints. All are part of the story.

In the same way it would be a mistake to think of Church history only in terms of the people at the "top"—popes, bishops, theologians, and other important people. On the contrary, Church history is also the story of countless ordinary people who make up the great body of the Church in every age. As we learn more about the lives and faith of these ordinary Christians—people like our parents, grandparents, and great-grandparents—we begin to see how our Catholic past can help us live our faith more fully in the present.

Jesus said that the kingdom of God is like a tiny mustard seed that grows into a huge tree on which all the birds of the air come to perch. Something like that can be said of the history of the Church. Someone once said that when you say, "Catholic," you are saying, "Here comes everybody!"

Places   In the ancient Greek translation of one of the books of the Old Testament, wisdom is said to have "pitched her tent" in Israel. People also "pitch their tents"—that is, dwell—somewhere. For that reason we can say that Church history is not only made up of people; it is also made up of places. These places may be very important and influential, or they may be quite modest. They may be very large, bustling cities; or they may be quite small, well off the beaten track. Whatever or wherever they are, they have each played some part in the great drama of Church history.

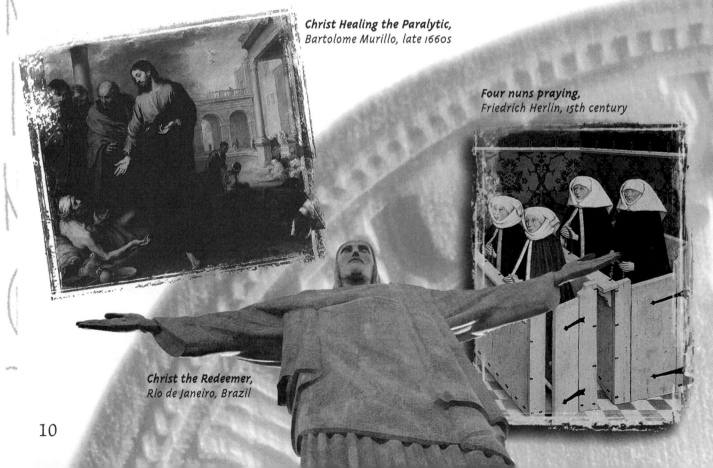

Christ Healing the Paralytic,
Bartolome Murillo, late 1660s

Four nuns praying,
Friedrich Herlin, 15th century

Christ the Redeemer,
Rio de Janeiro, Brazil

Buildings People like to build things. Since the dawn of recorded history some five thousand years ago, people have been piling stone upon stone or brick upon brick to make something useful. Sometimes the buildings that result express the builders' idea of comfort. Sometimes these buildings express pride in the builders' achievements, either as a nation or as individuals. Sometimes the buildings express deeply held religious beliefs and aspirations.

As we explore the record of Church history, we will encounter some of these buildings. Sometimes they will be huge and imposing structures like St. Peter's Basilica in Rome. Sometimes they will be little more than modest chapels. Whatever they are, these structures play a part in Church history because they record how people feel about their faith at a particular time and place in history.

Events People also interact with one another. The result of this interaction is often what we call an event, and Church history is filled with events. Some of these events are of tremendous importance—for example, the conversion of the Roman emperor Constantine (around 280–337) to Christianity on his deathbed or the beginning of the Second Vatican Council in 1962. Other events are more personal, more intimate, and more private—for example, the Blessed Virgin's appearance to Bernadette at Lourdes, France, in 1858. Big or small, events make up a large part of the great pageant of Church history down through the ages.

Ideas People also think. The result of thinking is usually an idea. It is therefore not surprising that part of Church history relates to ideas. Some of these ideas are difficult to understand—for example, the doctrine of the Trinity. Others are not so hard to grasp—for example, the mission of the Church. As we investigate the long history of the Church, we will encounter numerous ideas that have played a part in shaping our faith.

 What other topics besides those mentioned might you expect Church history to cover? Explain.

St. Peter's Basilica, Rome, Italy

And the future . . . ?

The Italian sculptor Michelangelo made his famous statue of Moses about 1515. What does it tell us about the way Michelangelo viewed this famous figure from the past? A historian would probably say that the statue is awesome and reflects Michelangelo's deeply held belief in the power and majesty of God, whom Moses served.

Tools of the Trade

How do historians go about investigating the past? Where do they begin? What tools do they use? Let's look and see.

One of the first things historians try to do is put themselves in the time period they are investigating. They do this by asking and trying to answer all sorts of questions about the people who were living at the time. For example, a historian studying the ancient Greeks might ask: What did the people of ancient Greece look like? How did they dress? What language did they speak? How did they earn a living? What kinds of buildings did they construct? How was their society organized? What sort of religion did they practice? How did they look at the natural world? What did they think about life and death?

Why are asking and answering such questions so important to historians? The answer is simple: Historians want to know how life was really lived at a particular moment in time. Because they want to see the past with the eyes of those who were living at the time, historians never read the present into the past. They let the past speak for itself.

To help them answer the questions they have asked, historians—including Church historians—regularly make use of certain "tools." These tools are not the kind we would normally find in a toolbox, but they perform a similar function: They help historians do their job.

Some of the historian's tools deserve our special attention. One of them consists of the physical remains of the past, including buildings and ruins, archaeological discoveries, and art. Another is the written record of the past, including documents and literature. Let's take a closer look at each.

Buildings and Ruins   The Colosseum is a world-famous landmark in Rome. In it the ancient Romans staged bloody gladiatorial contests, wild-animal hunts, and even naval battles for the amusement of the general public. It was here also that early Christians were martyred for their faith.

What does the Colosseum tell historians about the society that built and used it? For one thing, it tells historians that in Roman times life was not as precious as we consider it today. For another, it says that the lives of the very first Christians were often in danger.

The Colosseum, Rome, Italy

Archaeological Discoveries and Art

Archaeologists are hands-on historians. They investigate the past by literally digging it up with picks and shovels. It is exciting work. Take, for example, the discovery of the tomb of the Egyptian boy-king Tutankhamen in 1922. Imagine what it must have felt like to be the first person in over three thousand years to crawl into this tomb and see the splendid treasures it contained. This discovery and others like it forever changed our understanding of the past.

The *catacombs* are the ancient underground burial places of the early Christian community in Rome. They tell us all sorts of interesting things about the beliefs of our ancestors in faith. For example, they indicate that the early Christians had a deep reverence for the body, the temple of the Holy Spirit. The decorations show their belief in the hope of the resurrection. The way Christ is pictured also tells us about their love for him as the Good Shepherd.

Documents and Literature

It is amazing just how much of the past has come down to us in the form of written records. For example, the actual words of ancient pagan and Jewish historians who mention Jesus and his first followers can still be read. The works of a great many other writers, such as poets and great thinkers, have also come down to us, either whole or in fragments. These works tell historians a great deal about what the people who wrote them thought and believed and how they practiced their faith.

As we can see, the tools of a historian are many and varied. People who love history often find themselves in different places around the world where they try to imagine themselves back in time. There they look to discover the rich treasures of human experience. Church historians are men and women of faith who want all of us to get a clearer glimpse of God's activity in our lives. They show us our roots and help us understand who we are today by showing us the places from which we come. Historians are always in touch with life.

 What kinds of evidence might a historian hundreds of years from now use to study life in the late twentieth century?

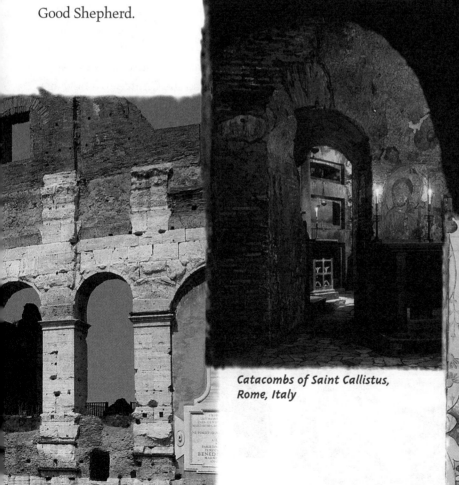

Catacombs of Saint Callistus, Rome, Italy

Page from the Book of Hours of Catherine Cleves, 1440s

Saints and Sinners

One reason Church history can be exciting is that we are introduced to our heroes and heroines—courageous men and women who have done so much for the Church and for the world. Sometimes, however, people who look into Church history are surprised to find that there have been a great many sinful people in the Church. They may even be shocked to discover that some of the Church's most famous leaders lived scandalous lives. Should historians try to cover up such things because they are not ideal or the way we would like them to have been? Just how should faithful historians look at the past?

Church historians are dedicated men and women of faith who are not interested in creating fiction. They are interested in presenting the facts as clearly and accurately as possible. When they find that some members of the Church lived sinful lives or made poor decisions, Church historians must always remember that the Church is made up of people, who are both saints and sinners.

They realize that the Church is human—sometimes all too human. At the same time, however, they know that the Church is also a divine institution because it is the body of Christ.

Sometimes in the history of the Church, we find people who were more interested in gathering wealth than in being faithful followers of Christ. Sometimes we meet people who were more interested in exercising power over others than in serving them. All too often we encounter people who were more interested in the things of this world than in the world to come. Do good historians ignore such people? Absolutely not. They are part of history, and facts are facts.

How should we look at such awkward facts? Should we be disillusioned about the Church? Not at all. Faith-filled historians realize that the mistakes of some do not change the true nature of the Church as Christ gave it to us. The Holy Spirit will still be active in the Church until the end of time. Even in the midst of difficult times in the Church, God raised up marvelous men and women to help lead the Church to a new age.

Pope John XXIII

Venerable Pierre Toussaint

Sister Thea Bowman

Dorothy Day

Blessed Junipero Serra

A Human Struggle

When it is carrying out its mission of preaching the word of God and dealing with all that God has revealed to us, the Church enjoys God's special help. This is the safeguard that Christ promised us through the presence of the Holy Spirit. But Jesus did not promise that the history of the Church would be an easy one or that the Church would be right in areas not properly its own—for example, in questions of science. One of the most famous examples of poor judgment on the part of Church authorities involved the scientist Galileo.

For centuries people had believed that planet Earth was the center of the whole universe and that the Sun and all other heavenly objects revolved around it. During the seventeenth century the Italian astronomer Galileo helped people to realize that they were not the center of the universe. This news was unsettling to many. People in the Church thought that this scientific evidence contradicted what they read in the Bible. For that reason Church authorities condemned Galileo and his ideas. It was not until the twentieth century that Pope John Paul II admitted that Church authorities had been wrong. A faulty decision had been made about a scientific matter.

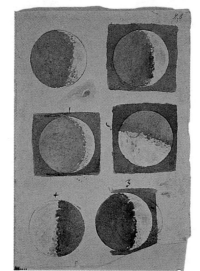

Phases of the moon, Galileo's drawings

How should faithful historians view the case of Galileo? Historians understand that the Church of the seventeenth century was subject to the scientific views of the time. While not approving of mistakes that were made in the past, historians try to understand why people made those mistakes. Historians remind us that people of every time are limited to the things and ideas that are available to them. For example, we do not expect early Christian writers to have been familiar with electricity or computers or modern biology. In every age people are products of their time. That is why historians are careful in their research and in their conclusions.

Catholics today know that we can only see the past by standing on the shoulders of men and women who have gone before us. We try to discover what their struggles were. Through their lives we try to find out the truth. This truth will make us better followers of Christ and better members of the Church today and in the future. That is why the study of history touches past, present, and future. It is ever ancient and ever new.

 Do people sometimes forget that the Church is both human and divine? Explain.

Mother Teresa

CATHOLIC ID

The Church considers a knowledge of Church history essential to a proper understanding of the Catholic faith. That is why courses in Church history are given at every level of Catholic education, from parochial schools and parish education programs to colleges and universities. In seminaries young priests-in-the-making are regularly exposed to Church history as part of their training.

things to think about

How do you think studying the past will help you understand the present?

Do you think that studying history will help you grow as a Catholic? How?

things to share

Should historians lie about or try to cover up unpleasant or embarrassing facts from the Church's past? Why or why not?

A friend says, "What's the point of studying Church history? It has nothing to do with real life." How would you respond?

WORDS TO REMEMBER

Find and define the following:

history _____

_____

_____

catacombs _____

_____

_____

OnLine WITH THE PARISH

Do you realize that you are already a part of Church history? The day you were baptized, your name was set down forever in the records of the parish in which you were baptized. In fact, historians often use parish records not only to trace family trees but also to discover the details of a person's life. A hundred years from now, your great-grandchildren may be looking you up in the parish records. Find out how records are kept in your parish and who is responsible for them.

What is the value of studying Church history?

1

Name and explain some of the things that make history.

2

What do the catacombs tell us about the early Christians?

3

What do we mean when we say that the Church is made up of saints and sinners?

4

What can buildings and ruins tell us about our ancestors in faith?

5

Life in the Spirit

When we talk about saints and sinners in the Church, we are not talking about "us" and "them." We are talking about ourselves because we are all a mixture of saint and sinner. If anything, Church history teaches us to be patient with other people's faults. As Jesus himself told us, "Let the one among you who is without sin be the first to throw a stone" (John 8:7).

CENTURIES OF AMAZING GROWTH

A.D. 30–313

Thy kingdom come;
thy will be done on earth
as it is in heaven.

The last thing Jesus told his disciples was to share the good news with the whole world. If you had been one of those first disciples, what might you have done to get your message across? What obstacles might you have encountered?

Growth of Christianity

Jesus appeared to his disciples a number of times after his resurrection to reassure them that he had indeed risen from the dead. These appearances and the gift of the Holy Spirit on Pentecost transformed the little group of frightened disciples into a community of enthusiastic believers who wanted to tell everyone about Jesus. The result was one of the most remarkable success stories that the world has ever known: the growth of the Catholic Church between 30 and 313. In this chapter we will see how and why this amazing development occurred.

The earliest Christians often said that God became Man "in the fullness of time." By this phrase they meant in part that during Jesus' lifetime and for several centuries thereafter, conditions were ideal for the growth and spread of Christianity. Some of these conditions deserve our special attention.

The Roman Peace During the early Christian period, all the lands and peoples of the Mediterranean world were united in one vast state under the control of Rome. The existence of this state, which we call the Roman Empire, made possible the conditions that helped Christianity to spread.

For one thing, the empire brought a good measure of peace and security to the lands and peoples it included. This whole period, in fact, was called the Roman peace. The government was for the most part stable, and order was maintained. Major wars were infrequent, and those that did occur were localized or fought well beyond the empire's frontiers. Rome's closest neighbors were weak and disorganized, so the empire's borders were secure. On the whole, people could breathe easily when it came to security. As a result it was safe to travel from one part of the empire to another, and this situation contributed greatly to the rapid growth of Christianity.

The Romans had a talent for engineering and soon developed a marvelous system of roads, bridges,

and harbors to link one part of the empire with another. This made travel not only safe but easy. Christian missionaries were quick to take advantage of this situation in their efforts to spread the gospel.

Cultural Unity   During the early Christian period, the Mediterranean world was unified not only politically but also culturally. This was due in part to the Macedonian king Alexander the Great (356–323 B.C.), whose conquests helped spread Greek culture throughout the eastern Mediterranean. When the Romans took over some of these territories, they continued to promote Greek culture as a unifying force.

One of the results of the spread of a common Greek-like culture was the development of a language that all citizens of the empire could understand. This common language, a simplified form of Greek, made it possible for Christian missionaries to speak to people all over the empire. That helped spread the gospel more easily.

Spiritual Hunger   Despite the blessings of the Roman peace, many people felt an emptiness in their lives, a kind of spiritual vacuum that the material benefits of the times could not fill. This atmosphere of spiritual hunger and the fact that people were generally willing to listen to all sorts of preachers greatly aided the rapid growth of Christianity.

The Christian Example   Jesus told his followers that by their love for one another they would show all that they were his disciples. Obedient to his words, early Christians showed their love for one another and for others in such ways as helping the poor, providing hospitality for strangers, and visiting the sick. Putting love into deeds, as one historian has observed, "was probably the most potent single cause of Christian success."

Finally, we should not overlook the most obvious reason of all for the success of Christianity— Jesus himself.

The Beginnings

Church history can be said to have begun in Jerusalem on the feast of Pentecost about A.D. 30. On that day the little group of Jesus' followers received the Holy Spirit, began to preach the good news to their neighbors, and attracted the first converts to Christianity. These converts were mostly Palestinian Jews who spoke Aramaic and who had little contact with the outside world. In fact Christianity at this stage seemed to be little more than a new form of Judaism.

Soon Greek-speaking Jews were attracted to the Christian community in Jerusalem. These Jews were different from the Palestinian Jews. They had not been born or brought up in Palestine. They had been deeply influenced by Greek culture. And they practiced their Jewish faith somewhat differently from the Palestinian Jews.

These differences soon led to tensions between the two groups of Jewish-Christians. To restore peace, seven men were appointed to help the Greek-speaking Jews, or Hellenists, enter the Christian community more smoothly. Unfortunately the tensions grew worse. Blood was shed, and the Hellenists were forced to flee north to Samaria or to the city of Antioch in Syria. Despite this, however, Christianity had taken a great step forward by including Jews from outside Palestine.

Once in Antioch the Greek-speaking Jewish-Christians began to spread the good news among the Jews outside Palestine. More important, they started to proclaim the gospel to Gentiles, or non-Jews. It was also in the city of Antioch that the followers of Jesus were for the first time called Christians (about A.D. 40). Not only was faith in Jesus slowly spreading throughout the area north of Palestine, but it was also becoming recognized as distinct from Judaism.

The entry of Gentiles into the Christian community caused another dispute in the Church. Jewish-Christians wondered whether these Gentiles had to become Jews before they became Christians. Opinions differed, and trouble appeared to be brewing. Fortunately the dispute was resolved peacefully.

About A.D. 48 Church leaders came together in Jerusalem for the first Church council ever held. Guided by the Holy Spirit, this council declared that Gentiles did not have to become Jews before they became Christians.

This ruling marked a milestone in the development of Christianity. For one thing, it made clear that Christianity was not just a form of Judaism but a religion in its own right. For another, it showed that the good news was not reserved for Jews alone but was for all people.

The result of the Council of Jerusalem spurred Church efforts to reach out to the Gentile world. Saint Paul was especially active in this field. Missionary journeys took him across Asia Minor (modern Turkey) and even to Europe (A.D. 50), where he established Christian communities in a number of cities in Greece. He even visited Rome (A.D. 63). Countless other missionaries were also preaching the gospel, so that by the end of the first century, Christianity had become well established in the eastern Mediterranean.

Then & Now

Have you ever wondered why recent popes have spent so much time traveling around the world? The answer is simple: Just as the apostles brought the good news to such places as Corinth and Rome, their modern successors are actively engaged in spreading the gospel to all nations. In this activity they are not alone. Countless other women and men are at this very moment also following in the footsteps of the apostles.

The Spread of Christianity

To the south and west of Palestine lies the land of Egypt. Here and along the North African coast, Christian missionaries sowed the seeds of faith. By the middle of the second century, Christian communities were present not only in Alexandria, the largest city in Egypt, and along the Nile but also in cities such as Carthage.

In the western part of the Roman Empire, the first important Christian community was established in Rome. Although this city is traditionally associated with Peter and Paul, the origins of the Christian community in it probably go back beyond these apostles to nameless missionaries who had visited Rome some years earlier.

In Gaul (modern France), Britain, and Spain, Christianity spread more slowly than in the East. By the middle of the second century, however, there were Christian communities in southeastern France. In Britain Christianity probably did not

make much headway until the middle of the third century. As for Spain there were Christian communities in such towns as Léon and Saragossa by the second century.

As a result of all this missionary activity, a network of Christian communities had grown up throughout the Roman world by A.D. 313. Jesus' command to teach all nations appeared to be well on the way to fulfillment, and Christians could feel justified in calling their community the Catholic Church. *Catholic* means "universal," and clearly the Church was at home everywhere along the shores of the Mediterranean Sea.

If you had been an early Christian missionary, how would you have gone about sharing the good news?

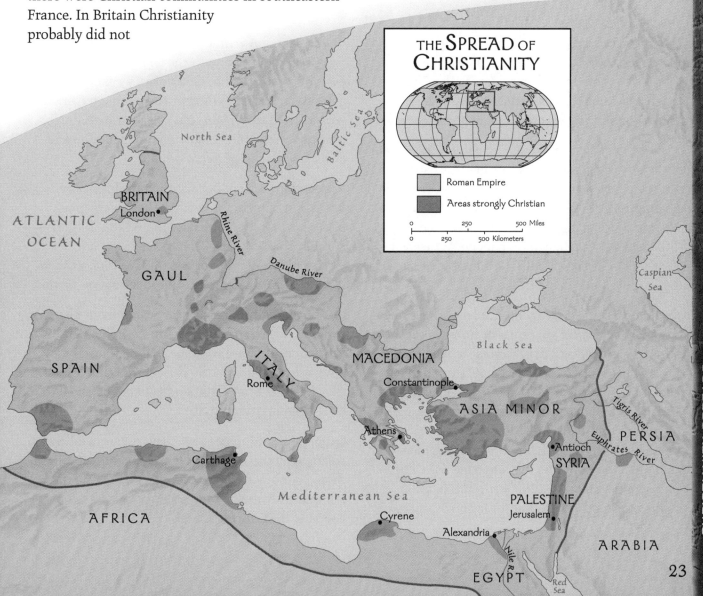

THE **SPREAD** OF **CHRISTIANITY**

Roman Empire

Areas strongly Christian

0   250   500 Miles
0   250   500 Kilometers

23

Christian Martyrs: The Last Prayer, Gerome, 19th century

Persecution

The spread of Christianity during the first three centuries of our era was a remarkable achievement. It was even more remarkable because the Church had to overcome serious obstacles just to survive. One major obstacle was the Roman government.

From the very first the Roman government viewed Christians with suspicion. In its eyes Christians were bad citizens who threatened the security of the empire. For one thing, Christians did not worship the pagan gods on whose favor the safety of the empire was thought to depend. Worse yet, Christians refused to honor the emperor as a god, and that was considered treason.

Christians also held frequent meetings, sometimes at night. The Roman government frowned on these meetings because past experiences showed that similar gatherings often led to discontent and rebellion. Rumors spread that at these meetings Christians took part in strange ceremonies, involving cannibalism and forbidden sexual practices. Both these charges, of course, came from misunderstanding the language used in the Eucharist and the early Christians' habit of calling one another "brother" or "sister."

The Roman government thought that such practices, combined with the Christian belief that everyone was equal in God's eyes, weakened public morality and state authority. Even though Christian writers tried to explain that Christianity did not pose any threat, misunderstanding persisted and eventually led to persecution.

Persecution was not one continuous three-hundred-year reign of terror, however. There were long periods when state officials ignored the Church, and Christians were relatively free from danger. Still, Christians were more or less outlaws and, as such, were always subject to hostile government action.

Curiously the first persecution came about almost by accident, when the emperor Nero blamed Christians for a fire in Rome that he himself may have started. Though the persecution that followed (A.D. 64) was brief, Peter and Paul are believed to have been martyred in it.

Other persecutions under other emperors followed. Fortunately these were brief and generally localized, though a number of famous martyrs, among them Ignatius of Antioch and Perpetua and her maid Felicitas, died during them.

Later Persecutions

Things changed for the worse in 250. Civil war, barbarian invasion, a drop in population, bad harvests, plague, inflation, and economic recession were at the time threatening the very existence of the empire. The emperor Decius (249–251) decided that the best way to hold the empire together was to force all citizens to worship him. Though Christians insisted that they were loyal to the empire, they refused to have anything to do with emperor worship.

Decius reacted very negatively to the Christians' response. He passed the first specifically anti-Christian laws the empire ever had, and he started the first empire-wide persecution.

This persecution was directed not at ordinary members of the Church but at its leaders. Its object was not to kill Christians but to force them to renounce their faith publicly; and Decius, through torture, made this a very easy process. As a result many Christians gave up their faith.

In 261 the emperor Gallienus passed a law tolerating the Christian faith; and for more than forty years, the Church was left largely at peace. Then in 303 the emperor Diocletian launched the worst attack on the Christian faith that the Church had yet seen. Though Diocletian's persecution did not strike all parts of the empire with equal force, it was so severe in some places that it came to be called the Great Persecution. Thousands were killed, Church property was confiscated, and sacred books and objects were destroyed.

Fortunately, in the western part of the empire, the Church had found a friend and protector in Constantius, one of Diocletian's corulers. He and his son Constantine made sure that the persecution was very mild in the territories they governed. In 312 Constantine became sole ruler of the empire in the West. In the following year he and his coemperor in the East issued a proclamation granting toleration to all Christians. This proclamation is known as the Edict of Milan. The Great Persecution was over, and a bright new day had dawned for the Church.

If you had been an early Christian, how would you have explained your faith to the Roman government?

PERSONAL PROFILE

Throughout the centuries faithful Catholics have given their lives for their faith just as the early martyrs did. Take, for example, Edith Stein (1891–1942), a German Carmelite nun of Jewish ancestry. After Adolf Hitler came to power in the 1930s, she asked to be transferred from her convent in Germany to a convent in Holland so that her presence would not give the Nazi government an excuse to persecute the other nuns around her. Once the Nazis conquered Holland in World War II, she was sent to a concentration camp and killed.

Ichthus, the Greek word for "fish," is made up of the initial letters of "Jesus Christ, Son of God, Savior" in Greek. The fish was therefore an easy and safe way for early Christians to identify themselves.

The Threat from Within

Along with persecution the Church faced another threat in the first three centuries of its existence. This threat came not from outside but from within the Christian community. It was directed not at people, as government persecution was, but at the Church's teachings. Because those who posed this threat often claimed to possess special personal knowledge unavailable to ordinary Christians, they and their followers were called *gnostics,* from the Greek word for "knowledge."

Gnostics were greatly influenced by ideas that were foreign to the teachings of Jesus. Some of these ideas came from Greek thinkers. Others were borrowed from popular religion or from magic and astrology. Still others derived from Judaism or from religions practiced by peoples living beyond the eastern frontier of the Roman Empire.

Many of the ideas that gnostics embraced were not new, but they were dangerous. That is because they had the effect of distorting the gospel message as proclaimed by the apostles and their successors. For example, some gnostics denied that Jesus was human, that he had been born of a virgin, or that he had died on the cross. Others denied that God was the creator of the universe or that the Old Testament had any value for Christians. Still others denied that the sacraments of Baptism and the Eucharist had any significance. Such beliefs totally contradicted apostolic teachings.

Needless to say, Church leaders reacted very negatively to gnostic ideas. As a result many gnostic groups broke away from the Church and set up their own separate little communities, much as cult leaders do today. The problem became so bad in the second century that not only Church unity but also its teachings were endangered.

The Church Responds

Church leaders were quick to respond to the threat posed by gnosticism. They realized that the only way to overcome it was to show that what the Church taught had authority because it was true and had been handed down from Jesus through the apostles. Gnostic teachings, on the other hand, had no particular authority behind them because they usually came from people who had no connection at all with Jesus or the apostles. On the contrary, advocates of gnostic beliefs usually claimed that their ideas derived from private revelations by the Holy Spirit or from special secret teachings of Jesus. Church leaders showed the falsehood of gnostic beliefs in a number of ways. Let us consider three of them: the New Testament, a rule of faith, and apostolic succession.

New Testament   As the Church spread throughout the Roman world, Christian writers of all kinds began to produce spiritual works to help believers understand and live their faith. Some of these writings contained the genuine teachings of Jesus as proclaimed by the apostles; others did not. As the gnostic threat grew, Church leaders began to recognize the need to distinguish between the two groups of writings. For that reason they began to create lists of works that truly reflected Jesus' teachings. These lists became the basis for compiling the New Testament.

By the end of the second century, the work of assembling the New Testament was well under way, though it did not receive its final form until the end of the fourth century. Possessing a body of Scripture that contained genuine tradition about Jesus greatly helped the Church to combat gnosticism.

Rule of Faith   Another way the Church tried to combat gnosticism was by providing a rule of faith. A rule of faith was very much like the profession of faith we recite every Sunday. That is, it was a short statement of the main beliefs of the Church. Having such a statement was very useful in the struggle against gnosticism.

Apostolic Succession   By the early second century, the leadership of the bishops was firmly established throughout the entire Church. The Church emphasized that these bishops could trace their authority directly back to Jesus and the apostles. This is called *apostolic succession*. This direct link guaranteed that the Church was passing on the true teachings of Jesus. The same could not be said of the leaders of the gnostic movement. Apostolic succession proved to be one of the Church's most powerful weapons in the struggle against gnosticism.

Eventually the Church overcame the gnostic threat. But while it lasted, the struggle was, as one historian remarked, "the hardest and most decisive battle in Church history."

 What modern ideas threaten Catholic beliefs? What can you do to combat such ideas?

CATHOLIC ID The earliest Christians possessed no special buildings in which to worship—no churches, basilicas, or cathedrals like those we are familiar with today. Instead Christians met in an enclosed place in the open air or in one another's houses. One such "house church" still survives. It was built in Dura-Europos (in Iraq) about A.D. 250.

PUTTING IT TOGETHER

things to think about

Do people today still experience the kind of spiritual hunger citizens of the Roman Empire felt so long ago? Why or why not? What would you advise such people to do to satisfy their hunger?

What would you do if you were faced with government persecution for your religious beliefs?

things to share

Suppose someone told you that he or she possessed special teachings of Jesus that no one else knew about. How would you respond to that person?

Jesus said his followers would show that they were his disciples by their love for one another. How can you and your group do this today?

WORDS TO REMEMBER

Find and define the following:

apostolic succession _____
_____
_____

gnostics _____
_____
_____

OnLine
WITH THE PARISH

How much do you know about the beginning of your parish? When was it founded? Why was it established? Who was the first pastor?

Team up with other members of your group to find out the answers to these and other questions. Then organize the information you have collected into a short talk and get permission to present the talk to a parish group of young people.

What conditions favored the growth of the Church during the first three centuries of its life?

1

How did the Council of Jerusalem contribute to the development of the early Church?

2

Why did the Roman government persecute the early Church?

3

Why were gnostic beliefs so dangerous to the early Church?

4

Why was apostolic succession so important?

5

Life
in the Spirit

From the very beginning Christianity has been a missionary religion. How can we tell non-Christians about Jesus and his message without offending them or appearing to be disrespectful of their religious beliefs? Find a quiet place in which to reflect on this question. Then frame your reflections into a prayer to help all those engaged in proclaiming the good news to the ends of the earth.

Faith
of an Empire
A.D. 313–476

CHAPTER 3

To worship in the Spirit, then, is to
have our minds open to the light.
Saint Basil the Great

Collapse of the Berlin Wall, 1989

Do you know what a turning point is?
Have you ever experienced one in your life?

A Turning Point

The year 1989 may be remembered as a major turning point in the history of the modern world. In that year the Communist empire in Eastern Europe collapsed, the Berlin Wall came tumbling down, and the Soviet Union ceased to exist. This sudden turn of events took many people by surprise. They never expected to live long enough to see the dawn of such a happy new day.

In the ancient world the year 313 was as big a turning point as 1989 may prove to be. That is because in 313 state persecution of Christians finally came to an end. Christianity, like the other religions practiced in the empire, was now officially tolerated by the Roman government. That meant that for the first time Christians could practice their faith freely. Christianity now enjoyed the same rights and protections under the law as the other religions of the empire. What an exciting time this must have been for all Christians!

Like the sudden turn of events in 1989, the Roman government's change of heart in 313 took most Christians by surprise. It occurred only about ten years after the emperor Diocletian launched the worst persecution of Christians the Church had ever endured. In fact, in some parts of the empire, the persecution had ceased only a little while before Constantine and his coemperor issued the edict of toleration (the Edict of Milan). Christians everywhere rejoiced at the news of the edict. Some even saw the hand of God working through the course of events.

Soon things got even better for the Church. Constantine not only stopped the persecution of Christians but also showed a marked favoritism toward the Church. This happened even though Constantine himself was not yet a Christian. His attitude was the direct result of his deeply held belief that his victories over his rivals for power were due to God's intervention.

One of the ways Constantine showed his preference for Christianity was by putting legal restrictions on the way pagans could worship. In particular he forbade certain non-Christian practices. These included the use of magic and the custom of predicting the future by studying the internal organs of animals or the flight of birds.

Most of Constantine's successors continued his policy. In 356 his son Constantius forbade animal sacrifices and closed most pagan temples. He also imposed the death penalty on those who disobeyed his orders. In 380 the emperor Theodosius I made Christianity the official religion of the empire. He followed this up in 392 by outlawing all pagan religions whatsoever. As a result of these last two decisions, Christianity ceased to be just one of a number of religions tolerated by the government and became the only one allowed by the state.

The fourth century after Christ was a major turning point in the history of the Church. This is because Christianity was transformed from being outlawed and persecuted into the only religion of a vast and powerful empire. What the Church realized from the experiences of the fourth century was that it did not live in a vacuum. It was in the world but not of it. It would always be affected, both positively and negatively, by the world in which it found itself. Jesus knew this very well. After all, he said, "Repay to Caesar what belongs to Caesar and to God what belongs to God" (Luke 20:25). In this chapter we shall look at some of the results, both good and bad, of this development.

Do you think people today take the freedom to practice their religion too much for granted? Why or why not?

Ruins of the Temple of Hadrian in Ephesus, Turkey

Some Pluses

The favor Christianity enjoyed under Constantine and all but one of his successors proved a mixed blessing. It brought the Church many advantages, but it also had some negative results.

Constantine was exceptionally generous to the Church. He gave it many buildings for public worship and other uses. He and his successors also built magnificent new churches, especially in Constantinople, the Christian empire's new capital (located in modern-day Turkey). As a result of all this activity, a distinctive church architecture developed.

In 325 Sunday was declared a holiday and a day of rest. In practical terms this meant that the law courts were closed on that day, so no official business could be transacted. A little later other Christian feasts—for example, Christmas and Easter—were declared holidays. Soon the everyday world of the Christian empire was moving to the rhythm of the Church calendar.

The rich Catholic tradition of helping the less fortunate that saw its first flowering in the fourth century continues today all over the world.

One of the most important organizations involved in this work is Catholic Charities USA. Founded in 1910, this agency aims at advancing the work of Catholic charitable programs throughout the United States. By the mid-1990s almost fifteen hundred groups were receiving its help.

Constantine and most of the other emperors of the fourth and early fifth centuries gave the clergy important new rights and privileges, as well as financial support. Clerics were excused from military service and from the obligation to spend a certain amount of time every year laboring on state-sponsored public works projects. Bishops were given authority in civil matters, especially in matters that concerned the poor. In fact bishops were considered the equivalents of provincial governors and given the appropriate respect.

In 380 Theodosius I decreed that clerics who had been accused of civil crimes could only be tried in a Church court, where penalties were milder. Laws also made it possible for ordinary citizens of the empire to leave lands and other valuables to the Church in their wills. As a result the Church grew rich and powerful.

The Church also influenced the way in which the state conducted business. In particular the Church saw to it that Roman civil law was brought more into line with the teachings of Jesus. As a result of the Church's influence, the practice of killing unwanted babies, child abuse, and gladiatorial fights were outlawed. Laws were enacted to humanize the treatment of slaves and prisoners.

The central nave of the church of Santa Maria Maggiore (St. Mary Major), built 432–440

Arch of Constantine, Rome, Italy

And divorce was tightly regulated. In addition the Church established a huge network of charitable institutions. Hospitals for the sick, homes for the poor and the old, orphanages, and inns for travelers were set up throughout the empire. Almsgiving— that is, the practice of giving of money and goods to support the less fortunate— also flourished.

And a Minus

Unfortunately imperial favor also had one major drawback. Because Constantine was not himself a Christian until almost the end of his life, he viewed the Church in much the same way as earlier pagan emperors had looked upon the old Roman state religion. That is, he regarded the Church as just another government department of which he, the emperor, was the head. After all,

Constantine the Great

Constantine reasoned, wasn't he the *pontifex maximus*, or "supreme bridge builder," the title traditionally given to a Roman emperor as head of the state religion? And if he was the head of the Church, wasn't he the equal, not just of bishops, but of the pope himself?

Today we call Constantine's exalted idea of his role in the Church *caesaropapism*. This term, which literally means "caesar is pope," indicates a view of Church-state relations in which supreme power in both Church and state is in the hands of a lay ruler—that is, a ruler who is not a member of the ordained clergy and perhaps not even a member of the Church.

Constantine's attitude caused the Church many problems. He insisted on exercising powers that properly belonged to the bishops. He repeatedly interfered in Church affairs, both great and small. And he generally tried to control all aspects of Church life. Because most of his successors adopted his policy, there was constant friction between the government and the Church. The collapse of the empire in the West in 476, however, brought a temporary end to the problem in western Europe. In the East, on the other hand, where the empire lasted until 1453, caesaropapism survived much longer.

What would happen today, do you think, if a civil leader attempted to run the Church?

35

The vision of Saint Augustine, Carpaccio, 16th century

Understanding the Faith

The favor the Church enjoyed during the fourth century made it possible for Christians in all parts of the empire to discuss their faith freely and in peace. Of course such discussions had been going on since the days of the apostles. But the new security the Church enjoyed provided Christian thinkers with the ideal environment in which to reflect on and write about the gospel message. The contribution these early Christian thinker-writers made to our basic understanding of Catholicism was so profound that they are to this day honored as the *Fathers of the Church*.

As a group the Fathers were witnesses of the ancient Church. They lived, however, at different times and in different places. The earliest Fathers lived around the end of the first century, and the last died in the seventh or the eighth century. For the most part the Fathers wrote in Latin or Greek, though other languages were also used. The body of writings the Fathers produced is called patristic literature, from the Latin word for "father," and the study of these writings and their authors is called patristics.

The Fathers were some of the most learned people of their times. They devoted their lives to reflecting on and writing about the meaning of the life, ministry, and teachings of Jesus. Their insights and the language they developed to express those insights are still a vital part of our Catholic heritage. The Fathers were also courageous individuals. They were pioneers because they had to provide the first answers to important questions about our faith.

The Early Fathers

The earliest Fathers of the Church are known as *Apostolic Fathers* because they are thought either to have known the apostles or to have been taught by the apostles' immediate successors. About the year 95 one of the Apostolic Fathers, Clement of Rome, wrote a letter to the Christians of Corinth to settle a dispute they were having. Clement's letter is the oldest evidence we have of a local Christian community looking to the Church of Rome for guidance.

A second group of early Fathers, who lived in the second century, are known as *Apologists*, from the Greek word for "defense." These Fathers wrote works explaining and defending the Christian faith. One of them, Justin Martyr (about 100–165), addressed several eloquent defenses of Christianity to the emperor and, as his name indicates, died for his faith. Another, Irenaeus of Lyons (about 130–200), defended the beliefs of the Church from the attacks of gnostic groups.

During the third century Christian writers attempted to gain a better understanding of their faith. They also tried to express this understanding of their faith in the best way possible and as clearly as possible. Among the Fathers who were most active at this time were:

- Origen (about 185–254), a scholar from Alexandria, Egypt, who spent his life studying and explaining Scripture
- Tertullian (about 155–222), a North African who provided Latin with a vocabulary to express the truths of the Christian faith.

A Golden Age

The golden age of the Church Fathers lasted from about 325 to about 451. The writers of this period were able to combine their deep understanding of Church teachings with broad general learning and extraordinary literary ability to produce a truly memorable library of writings.

The writers active during this golden age are far too numerous for us to consider individually. A few, however, deserve our special attention:

- John Chrysostom ("Golden-Mouthed") (about 347–407), a native of Antioch in Syria who later became known as the greatest preacher of the Church in the East
- Augustine (354–430), bishop of Hippo in North Africa, who struggled many years before he converted to Christianity and then became one of its greatest champions
- Jerome (about 347–420), a colorful and fiery scholar who is best remembered for the Vulgate, his translation of the Bible into Latin.

These and other early writers gave the Church a whole library of works that have been a guide and an inspiration to thinkers of every age.

 What one issue do you think the Church Fathers would want to write about today?

PERSONAL PROFILE

Before he was martyred, Ignatius of Antioch wrote a letter to some influential Romans who were pleading his cause before the emperor. He begged them not to do so. In 110 he wrote, "I beg you, do not interfere. Let me be given to the wild beasts, for through them I can reach God. I am God's wheat, and I am to be ground by the teeth of wild beasts that I may be found to be pure bread for Christ" (*Letter to the Romans*, 4).

Mosaic of three Church Fathers: Basil, John Chrysostom, Gregory

An Age of Councils

As Christian thinkers explored all aspects of their faith more deeply during the fourth and fifth centuries, disagreements in regard to individual points of belief started to arise. Such conflicts caused crises in the Church. To deal with these problems, important Church gatherings of all the bishops were held. Four of these gatherings are called ecumenical, or general, councils: Nicaea, Constantinople, Ephesus, and Chalcedon.

Nicaea   The first dispute to cause a crisis in the Church occurred early in the fourth century. It concerned the proper way to express the Church's teaching about Jesus, who is both God and Man.

An Alexandrian priest named Arius tried to give an explanation of the incarnation—that is, the taking on of flesh by the Son of God. Arius taught that God the Son was really a creature like ourselves, not the second Person of the Blessed Trinity. At the incarnation, therefore, God did not become Man; only a heavenly creature became Man. According to Arius, then, Jesus was not really divine; he was only human.

At first the bishop of Alexandria condemned Arius's teaching. Arius, however, ignored the condemnation. As a result there was turmoil in the Church and unrest throughout the empire.

To settle the controversy, Constantine called a meeting of all the bishops of the Church. This meeting took place in 325 in Nicaea, a little town not far from Constantinople. It was the first ecumenical council the Church ever held.

About three hundred bishops attended the Council of Nicaea. They rejected Arius's teaching as heresy. That is, they declared that it was wrong because it was contrary to God's revelation. In order to make the correct teaching clear, the bishops drew up a creed, or profession of faith. One clause in this creed stated that the Son of God was "one in Being with the Father." At the incarnation, therefore, God became Man.

Council of Constantinople, Cesare, 16th century

Constantinople Unfortunately the Council of Nicaea did not end the Arian heresy. To put the matter to rest, the emperor Theodosius I called another ecumenical council in 381. This time the meeting was held in Constantinople.

The bishops who attended the Council of Constantinople reaffirmed the acts of the Council of Nicaea. They also gave final form to the creed. This is the creed we proclaim at Mass every Sunday.

Ephesus Soon another question that caused a controversy came up: After the incarnation was Jesus two persons, a divine person and a human person? Or was he one person, and if so, was he a human person or a divine person? The followers of Nestorius, the bishop of Constantinople, mistakenly thought that Jesus was a human person in whom God was "housed." This implied that Jesus was two persons: a divine person and a human person— like flowers in a vase (a divine person inside a human person).

To set things straight, Nestorius himself asked that a Church council answer the question. The Council of Ephesus was called in 431. That council condemned any teaching that would split Christ into two persons. Ever since that time the Church has clearly taught that Jesus is one Person: a divine Person with two natures (a divine nature and a human nature). At the incarnation the second Person of the Trinity took on a human nature, not another person.

Chalcedon One more major religious controversy occurred before the empire in the West collapsed in 476. This time it was instigated by a very old monk in Constantinople who went to the opposite extreme of his predecessors. He began to teach that Jesus was not fully human.

A fourth ecumenical council, held at Chalcedon in 451, rejected the monk's views. It also put the finishing touches on the Church's teachings about Jesus by declaring that Jesus' divine and human natures were united in one divine Person.

The four councils we have been looking at established for all time the Church's teachings about Jesus. They also pioneered the use of the ecumenical council as a means of resolving doctrinal disputes. Their influence is still felt today.

A well-meaning person tells you that Jesus is not God; he was just a very good man. How do you respond?

CATHOLIC ID

It is important to understand that as Catholics we do not pick and choose what we will believe or not believe. We rely on the Holy Spirit to guide the Church, and it is through the Church that the understanding of the faith is expressed most clearly. Jesus promised the apostles, "The Advocate, the holy Spirit that the Father will send in my name—he will teach you everything and remind you of all that [I] told you" (John 14:26).

things to think about

The earliest Fathers of the Church had to be imaginative and resourceful when writing about their faith. After all, they had no written sources to which they could refer except Scripture. If you could ask those early Fathers about their greatest challenges, what would your question be?

things to share

What would you reply to someone who claimed that Constantine did nothing but good for the Church?

Why is it important for the Church to proclaim the creed? What is the value of the creed in your life?

WORDS TO REMEMBER

Find and define the following:

caesaropapism _____

_____

_____

Apostolic Fathers _____

_____

_____

OnLine
WITH THE PARISH

There are many turning points in the history of a parish. Think about your parish for a moment and the ways in which it grows and changes in each successive year. Think, too, of the many people who have come and gone in its service over the years. What do you think your parish can do to welcome new people who come to serve it?

Why is the fourth century considered such a turning point in the history of the Church?

1

Name one way that Constantine and his successors showed favor to the Church.

2

How did the Church influence the way Constantine and his successors ruled the empire?

3

What do we mean when we say that a certain person is one of the Fathers of the Church?

4

Choose one of the first four ecumenical councils, and tell why it is important in the history of the Church.

5

Life in the Spirit

Every year thousands of new religious books are published. Most of them are soon forgotten. However, some of the works of the Fathers of the Church have been in circulation for over fifteen hundred years. Have you ever thought of reading a classic such as the *Confessions* of Saint Augustine or the *Ecclesiastical* (Church) *History* of Eusebius? You may be pleasantly surprised to discover that books that are so old can be so interesting.

41

CHAPTER 4

TRIALS AND
NEW BEGINNINGS
A.D. 476–1054

You do not climb a mountain
in leaps and bounds,
but by taking it slowly.
Pope Saint Gregory the Great

When the winter snows melt, water levels may rise, often causing the swollen rivers to burst their banks. What kind of a challenge do you think this offers to the people who live along these rivers?

Invasions from Many Sides

In the fifth century the Roman Empire faced a great challenge along two of its rivers, the Rhine and the Danube, that formed the northern boundary of the empire. In earlier times the Romans built walls on their side of those two rivers and stationed soldiers there, not for the purpose of flood control, but for protection. They wanted to protect the empire from invasion by the peoples who lived on the other side of the rivers, the fierce Germanic tribes whom the Romans called barbarians.

For many years this defense system worked. But gradually the power of the Roman Empire began to decline, and the Roman legions could no longer safeguard the long northern frontier. More and more Germanic tribes crossed the border and occupied large sections of the empire, both in Europe and in North Africa.

As a result of these constant invasions, the once powerful empire had more or less disappeared in the West by about the year 500. The rich province of Gaul (modern France) had been conquered by the Franks. Spain was invaded by the Visigoths, another Germanic tribe. In 476 a king of the

Ostrogoths, yet another Germanic tribe, seized power from the last emperor in the West and established his own kingdom in Italy. In England Anglo-Saxon invaders from the area around Holland and Denmark overwhelmed the native British peoples, and in North Africa raiding groups of Vandals established a state that was little better than a pirate kingdom.

In the seventh and eighth centuries, a new and even more powerful threat came out of the East: the Muslim armies of Arabia. These soldiers were followers of Muhammad (570–632), a native of Mecca who had united the warring tribes of Arabia with his message of one true God, Allah. Fired by religious enthusiasm, the armies of Islam conquered much of the Middle East, all of North Africa, and most of Spain in less than a century. Such great Christian centers as Alexandria, Antioch, and Jerusalem fell to them. All this made travel and trading dangerous business around the Mediterranean Sea. The European economy was strangled, and Europe was isolated from the East.

As the Roman Empire disappeared in the West, many people wondered whether the Catholic Church would also disappear from western Europe. The barbarian invaders were not Catholics. Most of them were pagans. If the Catholic Church was to survive in western Europe, it would have to evangelize and convert these newcomers to Catholicism. That was not an easy task, however. The Church was centered in the great cities, but the barbarian newcomers lived in the countryside, far away from the major centers of Christian life. How could they be converted?

One solution came from a happy accident. At this time many Christians felt that city life, with its many worldly distractions, made it difficult for them to achieve the holiness to which they aspired. These Christians began to gather together in remote areas in religious communities called monasteries. In this way Christian monks came in contact with the pagan people of the countryside.

This almost daily contact provided the monks with many opportunities to share their faith with these people. As a result the monks became the great evangelizers and spread the good news of Jesus Christ during the period of history that we often call the Early Middle Ages.

 How do you think people felt as they saw their world of the Roman Empire gradually falling apart?

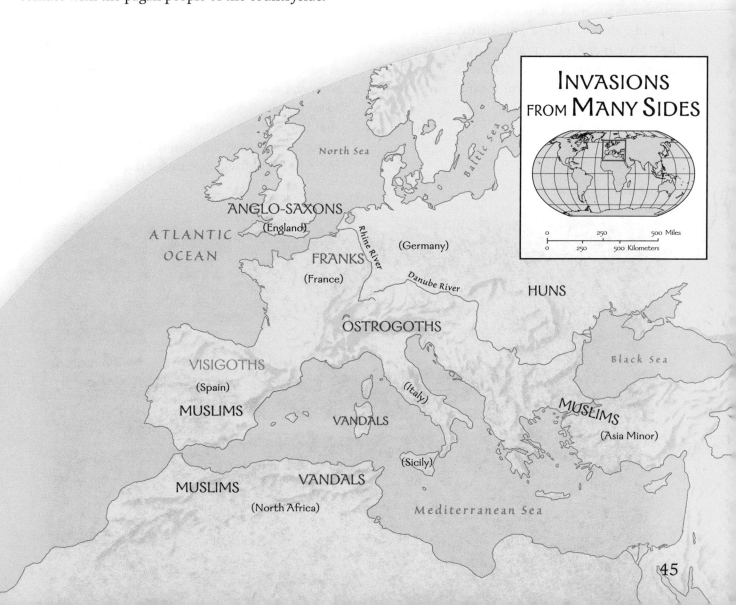

INVASIONS FROM MANY SIDES

North Sea

Baltic Sea

ANGLO-SAXONS
(England)

ATLANTIC OCEAN

Rhine River

(Germany)

FRANKS
(France)

Danube River

HUNS

OSTROGOTHS

VISIGOTHS
(Spain)

Black Sea

MUSLIMS

VANDALS

(Italy)

MUSLIMS
(Asia Minor)

(Sicily)

MUSLIMS
(North Africa)

VANDALS

Mediterranean Sea

45

Roots of Monasticism

Since the beginning of the Church, there have been men and women who wanted to dedicate their lives to the worship of God and to live the Christian life more fully. These are the people who founded the monastic movement, a movement that is still a vital part of the Church today.

In the fourth century Christianity became the favored religion of the empire. It began to attract all kinds of people. Sadly a few were more interested in using their membership in the Church to further their power and influence than in actually being faithful and dutiful followers of Jesus. The monastic movement was a grassroots response to this situation. It began among devout laypeople about the time of Constantine.

One such person was an Egyptian Christian named Antony (251–356). Around 271 he went off into the Egyptian desert to live a solitary life of prayer and deep thought. Others followed Antony's example, and soon there were many hermits in the desert south of Alexandria, living alone or in small groups in caves or huts. In fact that is what the words *monastery* and *monastic* mean: living alone, away from the world.

The monastic life proved to be so popular that it soon spread to Palestine, Syria, Asia Minor, and western Europe, where it produced many famous figures. By far the most famous of all the western monks was Saint Benedict (about 480–550). He lived and died as the abbot, or spiritual father, of a small Italian monastery called Monte Cassino, which he founded in 529. We know little about Benedict as a person. But he achieved lasting fame as the author of a famous rule, or guide to the monastic life.

Benedict viewed the monks in a monastic community as the members of a family under the guidance and direction of their spiritual father. The Benedictine motto, "work and prayer," reflected the fact that the monks' daily routine was divided between manual labor in the fields and community prayer at fixed times during the day and night. The Rule of Saint Benedict helped the monks to live the monastic life and was so well thought out that it was eventually adopted by monasteries all over Europe.

A monastery became in many ways a powerhouse of prayer and work. That is why it would be hard to exaggerate the wholesome and civilizing influence that Benedictine monasticism had on western Europe after the collapse of the Roman Empire. It brought unity to Europe under the cross of Christ.

Present-day Monte Cassino

Changing Times

There was one great weakness in Benedictine monasticism. Each monastery was totally independent. The monks in the community were accountable to no one outside the monastery walls. Therefore if the monks in a particular monastery became lax in their observance of the rule, it was difficult for any outsider to call them back to their duties.

In 910 a new monastery was founded at Cluny in France. There a series of devout and reform-minded abbots emphasized the need for prayer and downplayed the role of manual labor. Cluny soon gained such a reputation for holiness that hundreds of other monasteries affiliated themselves with it. As a result Cluny became the center of a huge monastic federation, and the abbot of Cluny became one of the most powerful officials in the Church.

The success of Cluny led in time to its decline. The abbey and its associated communities became large and wealthy institutions. Their prayers became very elaborate, requiring as much as eight hours to complete. Complaints grew that such monasteries were far from the small families of devout monks that Benedict had envisioned. The monks themselves cried out for a return to the "spirit of the desert." The result of this dissatisfaction was the establishment of a new religious order far stricter than the Benedictines.

Cistercian monk at prayer

The monastic movement is very much alive in the Church today. Monasteries can be found all over the world. Communities of men and women still follow rules of life that have been adapted for the modern age. Do you know of any monastic communities in your diocese?

The new order, the Cistercians, followed a very strict rule that combined a full routine of prayer and manual labor with little sleep and meager food. They built their monasteries in remote areas away from the distractions of everyday life. Despite the hardships recruits came by the thousands, many of them attracted by the leadership of Saint Bernard, who founded the Cistercian abbey at Clairvaux.

The variety of religious orders that arose in the Middle Ages and the ability of these orders to reform themselves were signs of the spiritual strength and creativity of the Christian monastic movement.

 What do you think the most challenging part of living the monastic life might be?

47

Evangelization of Europe

Why Europe? Why not the rest of the world as we know it? We must remember that at this time the known world surrounded the Mediterranean Sea. The Americas had not yet been discovered. Africa and Asia were mysterious places that were difficult to reach. The focus for the Church, therefore, was on Europe.

During the centuries after the collapse of the Roman Empire, the gospel was slowly spread to the barbarian peoples who lived in Europe. This task, which is called *evangelization,* was entrusted primarily to monks, who acted as missionaries; but popes, bishops, and laypeople also played a significant role. Let's take a look at some of the places that were evangelized.

France   One of the most important early steps in the evangelization of the barbarians was the conversion of Clovis, the king of the Franks. The Franks lived in Gaul, which today we call France. About 496 Clovis and his soldiers won a great victory over a rival tribe. Like Constantine almost two centuries before, Clovis credited his victory to God's direct intervention on his behalf. This led to the conversion of Clovis and was the beginning of an alliance between the Church and the rulers of

France. The result some centuries later was the founding of a new Christian empire in western Europe under Charlemagne.

Spain   The history of Catholicism in Spain began in 589 with the conversion of the barbarian kingdom of the Visigoths. Catholic Spain lasted for little more than another century, however, before Muslim invaders from North Africa conquered most of Spain. For centuries thereafter most Spanish Christians lived under Muslim rule. They struggled to regain control of their country, but the final Christian victory over the Moors did not occur until 1492.

Ireland   In Ireland Christianity became firmly established in the fifth century, thanks largely to Saint Patrick (about 389–461), whom the Irish regard as the apostle of their nation. Ireland soon became famous for its many monasteries, which were centers of learning and missionary activity. Some of the Irish monks traveled to

Saint Methodius,
Rasina, 18th century

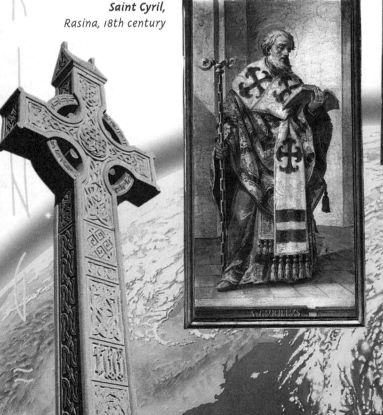

Saint Cyril,
Rasina, 18th century

Saint Boniface

were Saint Willibrod (about 658–739), who evangelized the Frisians in what is now the Netherlands, and Wynfrid (about 675–754), later known as Saint Boniface, the apostle of Germany. Boniface, with other Anglo-Saxon monks, established numerous monasteries throughout Germany. A century later a Frankish monk, Ansgar (about 801–865), began the evangelization of the Scandinavian peoples to the north, the Danes, Swedes, and Norwegians.

Eastern Europe   Among the most influential of all European missionaries were two Greek brothers, Cyril (about 827–869) and Methodius (about 825–884), who first brought the gospel to the Slavs of eastern Europe. The Slavs include such peoples as the Czechs, Slovaks, Croats, Serbs, Poles, Ukrainians, and Russians. Later in the ninth century, the invasion of the Magyars, or Hungarians, temporarily disrupted the Christianizing of the Slavs. After the coronation in 1000 of the first Catholic king of the Magyars, Saint Stephen, the evangelization was continued by missionaries from both East and West. The last peoples of Europe to become Christian, around the year 1200, were the inhabitants of the Baltic coast, which included the ancestors of the present-day Lithuanians.

By the year 1300 all of Europe was at least nominally Christian, from the sunny shore of the Mediterranean to the icebound coasts of Russia.

What qualities do you think a monk needed to bring the gospel to the barbarian peoples of Europe?

the European continent, where they helped spread the gospel in areas that had been devastated by the barbarian invasions. Other Irish monks, led by Saint Columba (around 521–597), went to Scotland, where they founded the famous monastic community on the island of Iona. From Iona a later generation of monks began to evangelize northern England.

England   In 597 Pope Gregory the Great sent Augustine, a Benedictine monk from St. Andrew's monastery in Rome, to convert the Anglo-Saxons, a Germanic tribe that had largely displaced the Celtic peoples in what is now southern England. Saint Augustine founded the first Benedictine monastery outside of Italy at Canterbury and converted King Aethelberht of Kent and his wife. Together the monks from Iona and Rome were responsible for the conversion of Anglo-Saxon England. By the end of the seventh century, all of England was Christian.

Germany and Scandinavia   With the encouragement of the pope, English monks carried the faith from their native land to the pagan tribes of Germany. Among these monks

When the countries of western Europe were being evangelized, the Mass was celebrated in the Latin language. Today the Mass is celebrated in the vernacular—that is, in the language of each country. Latin, however, is still the official language of the Western, or Latin, Catholic Church. Do you know any religious music that is still sung in Latin?

Coronation of Charlemagne, *from The History of the Emperors, 14th–15th century*

A New Christian Empire

The evangelization of Europe would never have occurred without the dedicated work of the monks. As we shall see, it would have been equally impossible without the guiding hand of the popes. It was the pope, for example, who forged an alliance in 754 with Pepin, the Frankish king. This paved the way for a new Christian empire in the West with Europe as its center and Catholicism as its creed. In fact this new empire would later be called the Holy Roman Empire.

By the eighth century the descendants of Clovis, the original king of the Franks, had become weakened rulers. In fact they were more or less under the control of lesser officials. One of these lesser officials was a very talented and far-thinking individual. His name was Pepin. He saw that the welfare of the Frankish kingdom demanded stronger leadership. Therefore he asked the pope to make him king. Why the pope? It is important to remember that during this time of the barbarians, the pope was one of

the few civilized leaders around. This is why he kept an army to protect the Roman people from attack. In fact all of western Europe looked to the pope for leadership.

The Lombards, another Germanic tribe, were a constant threat to Rome. In 753 Pope Stephen II turned to the Franks for help. He crossed the Alps and met King Pepin on Frankish territory. Pepin agreed to give the pope control over a large section of central Italy, a region that eventually became known as the Papal States. The pope recognized Pepin and his sons as rulers of the Franks and protectors of the Romans. The first steps in forming a new Christian empire in the West had been taken.

Before he died in 768, Pepin divided his kingdom between his two sons. When one of these sons died in 771, the other, Charles, became the ruler of all the Franks. As protector of the Romans, Charles soon had to go to Italy and fight the Lombards. This time Lombard power was crushed, and Charles, now called Charlemagne ("Charles the Great"), became king of the Lombards. Then, on Christmas Day 800, Pope Leo III set a crown on Charlemagne's head and declared him emperor.

Schism of 1054

While the Western Church's relations with lay rulers were improving, its relations with the Eastern Church were worsening. In 1054 a tragic split, or *schism,* occurred between the East and the West. This schism has lasted to this day despite efforts on both sides to heal it. Today we know the Western Church as the Catholic Church and the Eastern Churches that separated from it as the Eastern Orthodox Church. (The Orthodox Church is not to be confused with the Eastern Catholic Churches that remain in union with the pope.)

The Schism of 1054 came after a long period of tension and distrust between Christians in the West and Christians in the East. The causes of these tensions were mainly political and cultural, not religious. For example, many Eastern Christians thought Western Christians were ignorant barbarians. After all, the eastern part of the old Roman Empire had not been invaded by barbarians. Eastern Christians also resented the fact that the pope had crowned Charlemagne emperor of the Romans because this title was already claimed by the Eastern emperor in Constantinople. Further resentment was caused in the East when the Western Church added a phrase to the creed declaring that the Holy Spirit proceeds from both the Father and the Son.

Christians in the West watched with growing concern as the Eastern emperors, following the example of Constantine, tried to increase their control over the Church and even to extend that control to the West. Although the Schism of 1054 never completely healed, the Church in the West and the Church in the East share the same basic creed, moral code, liturgical tradition, and sacramental practices.

Orthodox Christians are our brothers and sisters in faith. See how much more you can learn about them.

51

things
to think about

Imagine yourself in one of the early monasteries founded by Saint Benedict. What would you enjoy about the communal life of work and prayer? What would be difficult for you? Do you think it is easier to live a Christian life in a monastery far away from the world or in the midst of it?

things
to share

Is today's world still in need of evangelization? Why or why not?

Share with others the ways you think the Church responded to the Holy Spirit's guidance during these many centuries.

WORDS TO REMEMBER

Find and define the following:

monastery _____

_____

_____

schism _____

_____

_____

OnLine
WITH THE PARISH

Like the Church at large, each parish grows and changes to meet the needs of the time. Name one way that young people can help their parish community to do this.

1 What part did monks play in the evangelization of western Europe?

2 Why did Saint Antony and other early hermits and monks choose to live apart from the world?

3 What parts did Clovis and, later, Charlemagne play in the Christianizing of Europe?

4 How did popes such as Gregory the Great become powerful civil as well as religious leaders in western Europe after the fall of Rome?

5 Briefly describe the Schism of 1054.

Life in the Spirit

The Catholic Church and the Eastern Orthodox Church have been separated for almost a thousand years. Use this prayer to pray for Christian unity:

Almighty and eternal God,
you gather the scattered sheep
and watch over those you have gathered.
Look kindly on all who follow Jesus, your Son.
You have marked them with the seal of one baptism,
now make them one in the fullness of faith
and unite them in the bond of love.
We ask this through Christ our Lord.

Amen.

CHAPTER 5

A Remarkable Age of Renewal

A.D. 1046–1305

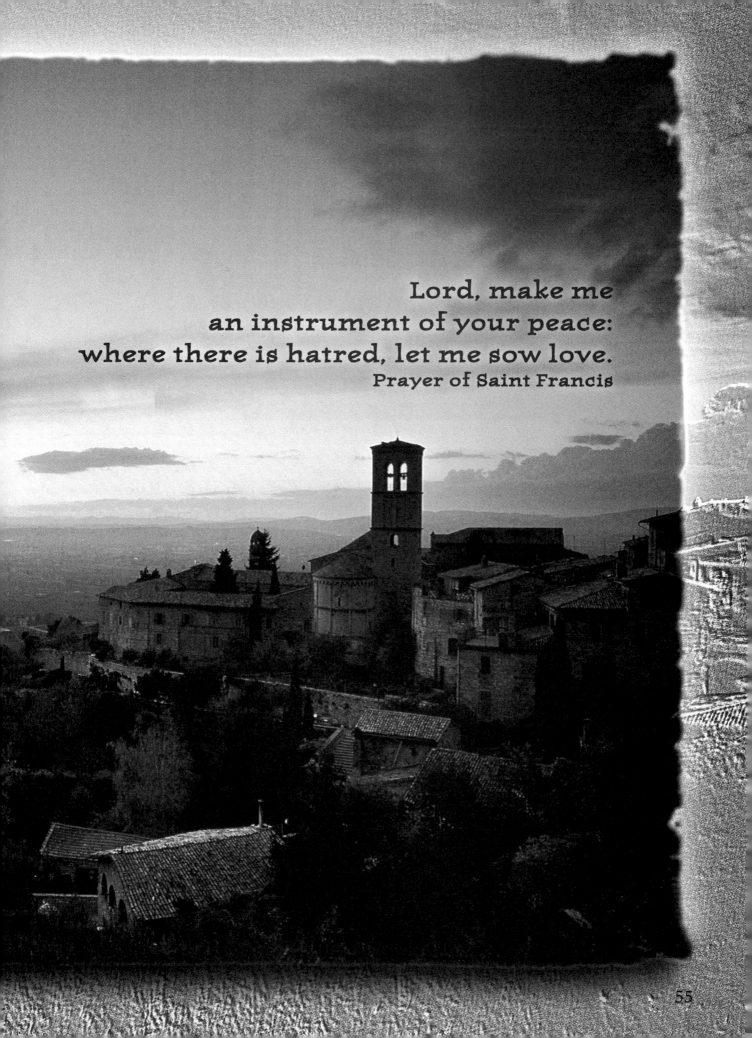

Lord, make me
an instrument of your peace:
where there is hatred, let me sow love.
Prayer of Saint Francis

Jesus Driving the Moneylenders Out of the Temple, Giotto, about 1305

Jesus once told his followers to reform their lives. What does the word *reform* mean to you?

A Need for Reform

One day Jesus went to Jerusalem and found the Temple filled with peddlers and money changers. What he saw made him angry because these people had no respect for the sacredness of the Temple. Jesus reacted by driving them out of the Temple. As we shall see, something similar happened in the history of the Church.

Throughout its existence the Church has often been in deep need of reform. In fact in the Church's history there have been times when several people claimed to be the pope simultaneously. Let's take a look at one of those times.

The year was 1046. The German emperor Henry III was visiting Rome and became very angry at what he saw going on. There he was shocked to find three rival bishops, each of them claiming to be the real pope. Each one was backed by a different family of Roman nobles, who wanted to make sure that the papal office and the wealth and power that went along with it stayed in that family alone.

The faithful emperor was so horrified by this display of power politics that he dismissed all three bishops and appointed the first of a series of German-born popes to replace them. One of these popes, Leo IX (1048–1054), began a reform movement that was to have a lasting influence on the Church.

Obviously the human element of the Church was in need of reform. The reform movement started by Leo IX reached a climax under Pope Gregory VII (1073–1085). In fact this reform takes its name from him: the Gregorian reform. It had the support of thousands of reform-minded clergy and laity all over Europe. Like Jesus in the Temple, these reformers were angry about the corruption of religion by money and waged a strong campaign against it. For example, they prohibited abuses such as the sale of dioceses and abbeys to the highest bidder.

56

The reformers soon discovered, however, that they could not achieve their goals until they solved a serious problem, the widespread practice by secular leaders (laypeople) of appointing priests, bishops, and even the pope. The reformers called this practice *lay investiture*. They said that it was an abuse that had to be stopped so that Church officials could be free to make their own appointments of priests, bishops, and other leaders.

The Gregorian reform movement was a complicated process that lasted almost seventy years (1054–1122). One episode that occurred in January 1077 will be forever famous. In the little Italian hill town of Canossa, Pope Gregory VII came face-to-face with the rebellious emperor Henry IV.

The pope had excommunicated the emperor and was on his way to Germany to urge the nobles to remove him from office. Being *excommunicated* was—and still is—a serious matter. This meant that the emperor could no longer participate in the sacramental life of the Church. To fight against this terrible sentence of excommunication, the crafty and clever emperor went south to Italy and met the pope at Canossa. For three days the emperor,

dressed as a penitent, stood in the snow outside the castle where the pope was staying. The pope lifted the excommunication but soon realized that he had been tricked. Henry returned safely to Germany but a few years later raised an army that drove Gregory from Rome.

In spite of some strong opposition, those who wanted to reform and improve the Church finally triumphed. In 1122 Pope Callistus II and Emperor Henry VI signed a treaty called the Concordat of Worms. This treaty, made in the German city of Worms, guaranteed the right of the Church to choose its own leaders without interference from emperors, kings, and other powerful laypeople. This treaty paved the way for a marvelous period of renewal in the Church. Catholics see an even deeper lesson in the whole story of the Gregorian reform movement. They regard it as one more indication that God never abandons his Church; he raises up good leaders even in the worst of times.

It has been said that the Church is always in need of reform. Do you think this is true? Why or why not?

Innocent III

With all that was going on in the world, it is no wonder that many people refer to this period of history as the High Middle Ages. The success of the Gregorian reform movement led to a vast increase in the power and reputation of both the Church and the papacy. As a result people all over western Europe began to look to the Church and to the pope to provide moral and spiritual leadership, especially through the application of canon law to the world at large. *Canon law* is the name we give to the body of laws of the Church. Remember that law and order were especially important to a society that had just emerged from barbarian times.

In the century after the Concordat of Worms was signed, almost all the popes were canon lawyers. The most famous of these was Innocent III, during whose pontificate (1198–1216) the papacy of the medieval period (Middle Ages) reached the height of its power. Though he was only thirty-seven years old when he was elected, Innocent was able to exercise an authority in both Church and state that few other popes have equaled.

To this day Innocent III remains a controversial figure in Church history. Some accuse him of trying to establish a theocracy in western Europe. A *theocracy* is a form of government in which all civil power is in the hands of the religious authorities. Others take a more favorable view. They see Innocent's actions as an attempt to give the Church a role in world affairs—not unlike that played by the United Nations today.

Probably the proudest moment in Innocent's life came during the Fourth Lateran Council of the Church, which met in Rome in 1215. Some twelve hundred bishops, abbots, and other Church leaders attended this council, at which almost every aspect of Catholic life was discussed and regulated by decree.

The Crusades

One of Innocent III's fondest dreams was the recovery of the Holy Land from the Muslims. Efforts to achieve this objective had been under way since 1095 and would continue, with varied results, long after Innocent was in his grave. Today we call the entire effort the *Crusades,* holy wars undertaken by Christians to win back the Holy Land.

The idea for the First Crusade came from Emperor Alexius I in Constantinople. He appealed to Pope Urban II (1088–1099) for help against the Turks, who were threatening the very existence of the Eastern empire. At the Council of Clermont in France in 1095, the pope issued a public appeal to the nobles and knights of western Europe to come to the aid of the Eastern emperor and to liberate

Then & Now

Even though the Fourth Lateran Council was held in 1215, many of its decisions still affect us today. It was at this council that the word *transubstantiation* was first used officially to describe the change of bread and wine into the Body and Blood of Christ at Mass. The council also made the rule that Catholics were to receive Holy Communion at least once a year.

the Holy Land from the Muslims. Thousands joined under the banner of the Crusade and headed for the Middle East.

Unfortunately the Crusade got off to a bad start. On the long march through central and eastern Europe, the undisciplined soldiers massacred innocent Jews. When the ragtag army of crusaders appeared before the walls of Constantinople, the frightened emperor urged them to move on quickly to the Holy Land, where they succeeded in taking Jerusalem from the Muslims in 1099.

The First Crusade was the only one to achieve any real military success, and even that was short-lived. Fifty years later, in 1147, the Muslims recaptured part of their old territory. This caused widespread dismay in Europe and led Saint Bernard of Clairvaux to organize the Second Crusade. Despite strong leadership, this Crusade was a total failure.

When the Muslims recaptured Jerusalem in 1187, a Third Crusade was organized. Despite the leadership of Emperor Frederick Barbarossa and King Richard the Lion-Hearted of England, it also ended in defeat.

In 1204 the Fourth Crusade, which Innocent III helped to organize, was not only a disaster but also a disgrace. Instead of attacking the Muslims in Jerusalem as originally planned, the crusaders turned against the friendly Christian city of Constantinople, which they captured and looted.

Later Crusades to the Holy Land were of no real military consequence. Yet for another five hundred years, popes periodically issued appeals for new campaigns. Few answered these calls, and Jerusalem remained in Muslim hands until 1917. Today we realize that the Crusades are an embarrassment to the Church because we know that the gospel should never be spread through violence or force.

Why do you think people tend to remember the bravery of wars like the Crusades rather than the violence and destruction?

Above: Detail from **The Battle of Antioch,** *14th–15th century*

Hagia Sophia (Holy Wisdom) in Istanbul (formerly Constantinople) is the largest surviving church of ancient times. It became a mosque in 1453 and is now a museum.

Saint Francis Preaching to the Birds, Giotto, 1320s

The Culture of Christendom

If one word could summarize the feelings and attitudes of this time in history, it would probably be Christendom. The word *Christendom* does not mean the same thing as the word *Christianity*. Christianity is the religion of the followers of Jesus Christ. Christendom refers to the cultural world that came into existence during the High Middle Ages in Europe. This was a period in which nearly everyone was Catholic and Catholicism influenced every aspect of people's lives. This does not mean, however, that everyone lived up to the teachings of the gospel in a perfect way. Let's take a closer look at several aspects of Christendom.

Threats from Within   Because all of society was based on Christian faith, that society would fight against anyone or anything that threatened the faith. Just as the Church fought outside threats during the Crusades, it also fought against inside threats such as false teachings or any other kind of opposition. Those who taught false doctrines were known as heretics, and their teachings were known as heresy. Sometimes even those who criticized the Church in a positive and faithful way were branded as heretics. Fear of heresy led to what has been called the Inquisition.

The *Inquisition* was an official Catholic court that was charged with examining and investigating those accused of heresy. It came into being in 1231. It not only examined heresy but also punished heretics. Sometimes the punishments involved imprisonment or fines. But sometimes it also included torture and death. Today it is not easy to understand how the Church in the name of the gospel could burn alive those who opposed it. Fear, however, can lead to many bad things, and the Church of the Middle Ages adopted the methods of punishment of that time.

The Coming of the Friars   The violence of the Crusades and the Inquisition were not the whole story, however. Many people wanted to help an all-too-powerful Church return to the foundation of the gospel. They wanted to be faithful to the example of of Christ.

Moreover, life began to change in western Europe. As a result of the Crusades, trade was increasing, and people were leaving the countryside for the new towns and cities that the revival of trade had brought into being. This shift in population soon

*Detail from **Saints Francis and Clare of Assisi**, 13th century*

led to the emergence of a new social class, the urban poor. Unfortunately organizations to provide for the material and spiritual needs of this new class did not exist in either Church or state. To fill the void, a new kind of religious order arose: the friars. The credit for this wonderful development belongs mainly to two very remarkable but very different people, Saint Francis of Assisi and Saint Dominic.

One of the best known of Christian saints, Francis (1181–1226) was the son of a wealthy Italian merchant. As a youth he dreamed of improving the world through deeds of courage and chivalry. After a brief and disappointing career as a soldier, he found life's meaning in the gospel message. He immediately gave up all his wealth and set out barefoot and penniless to preach love of God, joy in God's creation, and a sincere repentance based on trust in God's mercy.

Francis's strong personality and faith soon attracted many followers. He had no desire to start a new religious order, but the sheer number of his followers forced him to compose a simple rule to guide them. The pope accepted this rule and created the Order of Friars Minor. (The word *friar* comes from the Latin word for "brother.") The order became known simply as the Franciscans.

Another great order of friars was founded by Dominic (1170–1221), a Spanish priest. It was called the Order of Preachers, or the Dominicans. Dominic was moved by the desire to fight against any heresy that would mislead the faithful. To do this, he saw a need for well-educated and holy preachers who could explain the teachings of the Church and live according to the gospel. Dominic was impressed by Francis's commitment to poverty and simplicity. For that reason he included similar provisions in the rule he developed for his order.

Dominic did not have the magnetic personality of Francis, but he had other valuable gifts. He was a superb organizer, and he gave his order a strong structure that included elected superiors and a system of checks and balances. He also stressed the importance of education because he knew that a person must be well educated to be a good preacher. What an exciting period of history!

It has been said that God sends saints needed for the time. What kinds of saints do we need today?

Saint Dominic, *Fra Angelico, 15th century*

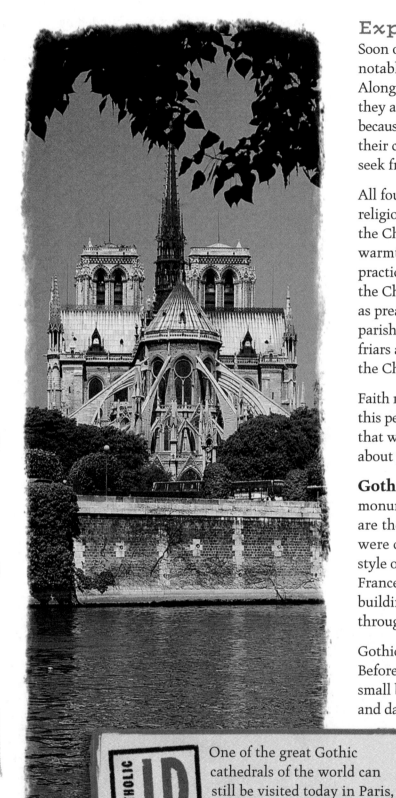

Expressions of Faith

Soon other orders of friars came into being, most notably the Carmelites and the Augustinians. Along with the Franciscans and the Dominicans, they are classified as *mendicant,* or "begging," orders because they emphasize personal poverty and finance their charitable activities from the donations they seek from the faithful.

All four orders had an immense impact on the religious life of the Late Middle Ages. They brought the Church closer to the people and added a new warmth to devotional life by introducing such practices as the rosary, the stations of the cross, and the Christmas crèche. They were highly regarded as preachers and confessors at a time when many parish priests were not trained for these tasks. The friars also taught at the new universities and gave the Church some of its most learned scholars.

Faith not only led to changes in religious life during this period of history but even affected the buildings that were built and the way that people learned about the world.

Gothic Architecture   The most lasting physical monuments of Christendom in the medieval period are the numerous cathedrals and churches that were constructed in the Gothic style. This was a style of architecture that developed first in northern France. Tourists today gaze in wonder at these buildings, thousands of which are still standing throughout Europe.

Gothic architecture became popular around 1150. Before that time churches tended to be relatively small buildings with thick walls, small windows, and dark interiors. Gothic architecture was different. Churches built in the Gothic style soared upward toward heaven as if reaching up to God himself. They were constructed entirely of stone, using the primitive construction machinery of the day. It required a great deal of engineering skill to build these Gothic churches without the aid of modern materials such as steel.

CATHOLIC ID One of the great Gothic cathedrals of the world can still be visited today in Paris, France. This is Notre Dame. The French word means "Our Lady" and reminds us that this medieval treasure was dedicated to the Mother of God.

Experts have shown that everything in such cathedrals fits together according to a master plan. For example, flying buttresses, which are outside supports for the walls of a building, are not just decorations. Rather, they are a necessary part of the structure, supporting the weight of the roof and walls and making it possible to insert large stained-glass windows in the walls. The windows themselves are designed to do more than just bring light and color into the interior of the building. They served as "sermons in glass" by illustrating important scenes and themes of the gospel message for those who could not read. That is why cathedrals have been called "living catechisms" and "the Bible of the poor."

Education and Learning   Even during the period of the sixth to the tenth century, known as the Dark Ages, the love of learning never entirely disappeared in Europe. Monks, copying manuscripts by hand, preserved the learning of antiquity and handed on at least the fundamentals of knowledge in the monastic schools, where they trained future monks. Bishops did the same in the cathedral schools, which they established for the training of the future diocesan clergy. In fact learning and education were practically a monopoly of the clergy and other religious during the Middle Ages.

One of the glories of Christendom was the establishment of universities, which made their appearance in the twelfth century. They were genuine centers of higher education. In them such subjects as law, medicine, philosophy, and theology were taught. These universities boasted of great thinkers—Anselm, Peter Abelard, Albert the Great, Bonaventure, and Duns Scotus—all of whom made lasting contributions to the understanding of Catholicism.

Thomas Aquinas (about 1225–1274), a Dominican friar, is perhaps the best known of all these medieval thinkers. He is important not only for what he wrote but also for his whole approach to learning. Unlike some other Christians, Aquinas was not afraid of knowledge, not even knowledge that came from the Muslim Arabs or from pagan Greek philosophers like Aristotle. Aquinas believed that "truth cannot contradict truth." Therefore, he said, reason can never really be in conflict with faith. Faith can take us further than reason, but the two can never be in opposition. If our faith tells us one thing and our reason tells us something different, he said, there must be something deficient in our understanding of the one or the other.

What does a medieval cathedral tell you about the faith of those who built it?

*Rose window
Chartres, France*

63

PUTTING IT TOGETHER

things to think about

Should we condemn the people of the Middle Ages for the Crusades and the Inquisition? Or can we say that they were acting according to the culture of their day?

Do you think it was easy for Francis of Assisi to live a gospel life during the Middle Ages?

WORDS TO REMEMBER

Find and define the following:

Crusades _____

_____

_____

Inquisition _____

_____

_____

things to share

What can the lives of people such as Saint Francis, Saint Clare, and Saint Dominic teach us about living our Catholic faith today?

Someone tells you that nothing good came out of the Church in the Middle Ages. What would you say to that person?

OnLine WITH THE PARISH

Look around your parish church, both inside and outside. How do its design and decoration help you to know about your faith?

What was lay investiture, and why was it important in the Middle Ages?

1

What does it mean to be excommunicated from the Church?

2

What was the main purpose of the Crusades?

3

Why were mendicant orders so important in the twelfth and thirteenth centuries?

4

What do experts mean when they say that Gothic churches and cathedrals are "living catechisms" and "the Bible of the poor"?

5

Life in the Spirit

According to an old story, one day Saint Francis of Assisi told a group of young friars that he would give them a lesson about preaching. He took them for a walk through a neighboring village, but he never spoke a word. At the end of the walk, the friars said to Saint Francis, "When are you going to teach us how to preach?" He replied, "I just gave you your lesson. What you are speaks more loudly than anything that you could say." How can you apply the moral of this story to your own life?

A Time of Crisis and Challenge

A.D. 1305–1517

Christ helps and strengthens us
and never abandons us.
He is a true friend.
Saint Teresa of Ávila

Have you ever felt that your life is a series of ups and downs? One week you feel you are on top of the world, and the next week you come crashing down! Do you think the Church community has its ups and downs, too?

Twilight of Christendom

It seems almost impossible that after the glories of the High Middle Ages, the Church and society would experience dramatic crises and changes. But that is what history is all about. It is about such ups and downs and about people and the choices they make. As we shall see, sometimes the members of the Church made wonderful and faithful choices, and sometimes they made disastrous choices. Even though the Church experiences ups and downs, we can still detect the presence of the Holy Spirit moving us forward. Let's take a look at this period of history that is both embarrassing and fascinating.

The period we are studying is often called the Late Middle Ages, roughly 1300 to 1500. Europe in these centuries fell short of the fragile ideals of Christendom. For much of the period, England and France were at war with each other, and Germany suffered under a series of weak and incapable rulers. In eastern Europe the militantly Muslim Turks captured the ancient Christian city of Constantinople in 1453 and then began to push their way into the heart of central Europe. By 1529 they had conquered all of southeastern Europe and nearly captured the city of Vienna. They were at western Europe's back door.

fervor that had been so prominent in the days of the Gregorian reform movement. In the universities theology had ceased to be the exciting field of study that it was in the days of Saint Thomas Aquinas.

In the parish churches fewer and fewer priests preached sermons on a regular basis or provided serious religious instruction for children. This was a major failure on the part of the clergy because few people owned books or could even read or write. As a result of this, some Catholics knew little about such basic matters as the meaning of the creed or the Ten Commandments. Some could not even recite simple prayers such as the Our Father or the Hail Mary.

Perhaps the most troubling thing of all was a lack of understanding about the real meaning of the Mass or the Eucharist. As we know, the Eucharist should be the center of every Christian's spiritual life. But in those years it became a vague and distant rite for many people. One problem was that few laypeople understood Latin, which was the language of the Mass, and so they got little benefit from hearing the Scriptures read during the celebration of the liturgy. Likewise, although it seems incredible to us today, even the most devout laypeople were allowed to receive Holy Communion only a few times a year. It is no wonder, therefore, that many people began to complain that the Church was not making good use of its own spiritual resources.

One other point needs to be mentioned. As Christendom began to weaken, the once all-powerful papacy began to decline. More and more, kings and princes would not tolerate the political advice or intervention of the popes. The members of the Church were beginning to understand themselves in a new way: as distinct from the state. They were beginning to see that civil governments were separate from Church governance. Amid all these crises and changes, there was still a feeling on the part of some that something new was happening. Changes were at work that would bring both confusion and deepening faith for many Christians.

It must have been scary to live at the time of the Black Death. What kinds of things frighten people today, and as people of faith how should we respond?

In those years Europe also experienced one of the worst natural disasters in its history: the so-called Black Death. This epidemic of bubonic plague swept like wildfire across Europe and left its victims blackened and disfigured. In some areas the plague may have killed as many as one-third of the population. The people must have suffered great fear and confusion. For many people there was nothing to think about other than death. Some must have felt that the world itself was falling apart.

This was also a dark and dreary period in the history of the Catholic Church. There were complaints that priests, monks, and nuns had lost the religious

The Avignon Papacy

Why did the leaders of the Church, especially the popes and bishops, do so little to correct the many things that were wrong in the Church in the Late Middle Ages? Unfortunately the popes and bishops were a major part of the problem. In fact there have been few times in history when the Church had such poor leaders.

From 1305 to 1377 the popes did not even live in Rome, although they are the bishops of that city. How did this situation come about? It began in 1305 when a French pope was elected. Instead of moving to Rome, this pope, Clement V, took up residence in the little city of Avignon in southern France. He appointed mostly French cardinals, and they in turn elected more French popes (no fewer than six of them between 1305 and 1377), who continued to live in Avignon.

The Avignon popes were not bad men, and they were not lazy or immoral. But they did the Church great harm by living in France, where they gave the impression of being under the thumb of the French king for all those years. As the head of a worldwide—that is, *catholic*—Church, a pope must be free from pressure from any ruler so that he can treat all people fairly. The Avignon popes failed to do this, and it caused many people in Europe to lose respect for the papacy.

In 1377 Pope Gregory XI left France for good and returned to Rome. A few months later Gregory died, and the cardinals elected a new pope, Urban VI. Most of the cardinals, especially the French cardinals, regretted their choice because the new pope turned out to be a tough reformer. One by one the cardinals slipped away from Rome and claimed that Urban VI was not the legitimate pope. They said that the Roman mob had forced them to vote for him because he was an Italian. They then held another election at which they selected an antipope, a nephew of the French king. This rival French pope took the name Clement VII. Unable to seize Rome, he returned to Avignon, where he established his own papal court. Now two men were claiming to be the pope. Adding to the confusion, Charles V, the king of France, recognized the antipope Clement VII and therefore confirmed the fact that there was now a schism in the Church.

The Great Schism

When Urban VI and Clement VII died, each was replaced by a bishop who insisted that he was the real pope. This state of affairs, which is known as the *Great Schism,* lasted for almost forty years, from 1378 to 1417. Everyone recognized that it was a scandal and wanted to put a stop to it, but it was difficult to know how to restore peace and unity to the Church. After all, Christendom was split in two, and both sides in the controversy tried to prove that they were right. Neither the pope in Rome nor the antipope would resign.

In 1409 cardinals and bishops from both sides tried to solve the problem. They held a council in the city of Pisa, Italy, and elected another antipope, Alexander V. He naturally expected that the two rival popes would then resign. But just the opposite happened. Neither the Roman pope nor the claimant in Avignon would quit. The situation was worse than ever: There were now three rival popes! Look at the chart to see how confusing this must have been for people.

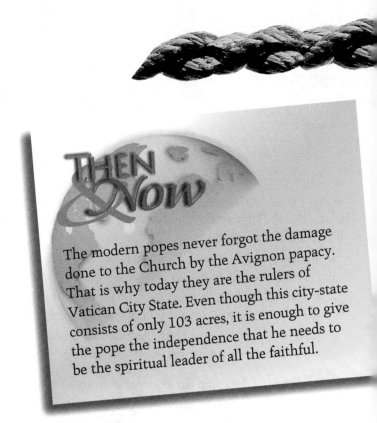

The modern popes never forgot the damage done to the Church by the Avignon papacy. That is why today they are the rulers of Vatican City State. Even though this city-state consists of only 103 acres, it is enough to give the pope the independence that he needs to be the spiritual leader of all the faithful.

Finally another Church council was held, this time in the Swiss city of Constance from 1414 to 1418. It was one of the grandest assemblies of the Middle Ages and has been compared with modern peace conferences. Holy Roman Emperor Sigismund was present, as were hundreds of cardinals, bishops, abbots, and theologians. In fact the attendance was so large that the participants had to be divided into five "nations": France, Germany, Italy, England, and Spain.

The Council of Constance finally put an end to the Great Schism. The Pisan antipope, John XXIII, turned out to be a man of weak character and was forced to give up his claim to the papacy. The Roman pope, Gregory XII, agreed to resign after he was allowed to convene the council, thus making it official. The Avignon antipope, Benedict XIII, refused to resign and was removed from office. This paved the way in 1417 for the election of a new pope, Martin V, who was acceptable to all sides. The schism was over!

Although the Council of Constance solved one problem in trying to reform the Church, it caused another. The council put an end to the Great Schism, but it claimed that general councils were now the supreme authority in the Church, superior even to the popes. This idea is called *conciliarism*. It is easy to see how such an idea originated during the crisis of the Great Schism. But the Council of Constance claimed this was the normal way that the Catholic Church should be governed. Pope Martin V refused to accept this claim, and later the Church condemned conciliarism.

What is the best thing to remember when we see the Church experiencing conflict and difficulty?

Popes and Antipopes
During 1378–1417

Popes of Rome
Urban VI (1378–1389)
Boniface IX (1389–1404)
Innocent VII (1404–1406)
Gregory XII (1406–1415)

Antipopes of Avignon
Clement VII (1378–1394)
Benedict XIII (1394–1423)

Antipopes of Pisa
Alexander V (1409–1410)
John XXIII (1410–1415)

The Renaissance

Beginning in Italy in the fifteenth century, Europeans rediscovered the culture of the ancient Greeks and Romans. Historians call this change the *Renaissance,* which means literally "rebirth." All over Europe scholars collected manuscripts that contained the writings of ancient authors. In painting, sculpture, and architecture, Europeans turned away from the styles of the Middle Ages and looked to the ancient Greeks and Romans as their models.

The Church is always affected by the changes taking place in the world, and the Renaissance had a profound impact on it, both good and bad. A major center of the Renaissance was Rome, where several popes made important contributions to the revival of classical culture and ideas.

Just as learning never completely disappeared even during the Dark Ages, neither did holiness disappear from the Church during the Late Middle Ages. In Italy, for example, in the early sixteenth century, reformers founded new religious orders to care for the sick and to preach to the poor. Saint Angela Merici brought together a group of women who later founded the Order of Saint Ursula, one of the largest educational orders in the Church. Among the old religious orders, there were also signs of renewal. The members of the Carthusian monastic order enjoyed wide respect for their fidelity to an austere way of life. In Italy a group of Benedictine monasteries formed a federation to promote reform.

The Renaissance also contributed to the currents of reform.

Christian scholars were interested not only in the cultures of pagan Greece and Rome but also in that of the ancient Christian world. They were eager to read the Scriptures in the original Hebrew and Greek instead of in Saint Jerome's Latin translation. They also searched through dusty monastic libraries for manuscripts by the Fathers of the Church. Thanks to the invention of movable type in the late fifteenth century, it was possible for the first time to print this enormous collection of writings instead of copying each work slowly by hand. Scholars called Christian humanists showed the same enthusiasm for this task as other scholars did for editing and publishing the pagan classics.

Humanists and Reformers

The Christian humanists were not hermits who spent all their time in libraries. Many were deeply troubled by the ignorance and corruption that they saw all around them. They believed that the key to reform of the Church was religious education, and they were especially eager to promote the better education of the clergy. They hoped that a renewed clergy would raise the general spiritual standard of the whole Church.

In England these Christian humanists included two future martyrs and saints, Thomas More (1477–1535) and John Fisher (1469–1535). Perhaps the most famous of the Christian humanists was Erasmus of Rotterdam (1469–1536), a Dutch priest and a friend of More and Fisher. Erasmus was both a scholar and an outspoken critic of abuses in the Church. In 1516 he published an edition of the New Testament with the original Greek text on one page and a Latin translation on the facing page.

Pietà, Michelangelo, 1498–1500

The Last Supper, *Da Vinci*

Another of his books, *The Praise of Folly,* was a stinging attack on corruption in the Church and a passionate plea for reform.

Still another outstanding Christian humanist and practical reformer was Francisco Cardinal Jiménez (1436–1517), a Franciscan friar who had been made archbishop of Toledo in Spain. Like the other Christian humanists, Jiménez combined a love of learning with a zeal for reform. He founded the University of Alcalá de Henares. He intended his university to be a training ground for future leaders of the Spanish Church, and he succeeded beyond his expectations. As we shall see, one reason the Protestant Reformation had little impact in Spain was that Jiménez had already reformed the Spanish Catholic Church. His influence reached across the Atlantic to the New World, where Spanish missionaries spread the gospel among the native peoples of Mexico and South America.

Unfortunately such dedicated men had only a limited effect on reforming the Church. They were able to reform individual dioceses or religious orders or even a whole country (in the case of Jiménez). However, they were unable to bring about the general reform of the whole Church because they met stubborn resistance from the papacy and many of the bishops. The Catholic Church cannot be reformed in any age if the popes and the bishops are not in favor of it.

Christian humanists said that the key to reform was religious education. Why is this still a good idea?

Construction of St. Peter's dome began during the Renaissance.

The Renaissance Papacy

Even though the Renaissance was a positive period of rebirth in art and learning, it also had a negative effect. Many people forgot the importance of faith and concentrated on human values. Even the popes could not escape this tendency.

The Renaissance papacy is usually dated from the pontificate of Nicholas V (1447–1455), who established the great Vatican Library. Unfortunately some of the later Renaissance popes took more interest in promoting art and architecture than they did in being the chief shepherds of the Church. Others used their high office to enrich the members of their families. Pope Sixtus IV (1471–1484), for example, conferred eight different dioceses on one of his nephews. That nephew later became Pope Julius II (1503–1513). Besides being the patron of the great artist

Michelangelo, Pope Julius was nicknamed "Papa Terribile" (the terrible pope) because of his fiery disposition. He personally led armies into battle and once celebrated a victory with a military parade through Rome on Palm Sunday.

The worst of the Renaissance popes was probably Julius II's predecessor, Alexander VI (1492–1503). This man fathered at least five children before he became pope and took more interest in the welfare of his family than in that of the Church. Another notorious figure was Pope Leo X (1513–1521). The son of Lorenzo the Magnificent, the ruler of Florence, Leo had been made a cardinal at the tender age of thirteen. When elected pope, he is supposed to have remarked, "Now that God has given us the papacy, let us enjoy it." He probably never made that comment, but he might well have said it. He, too, gave more attention to the fine arts than to his pastoral duties. In fact one critic said of him that "he had all the qualities needed for a pope except an interest in religion." Was it wrong for these popes to support the arts? No. Was it wrong for them to neglect the Church? Yes.

Bishops and Priests

The Renaissance bishops also left much to be desired. As in the days before the Gregorian reform, many of the bishops were appointed by kings and nobles. Frequently they had little sense of vocation to be spiritual leaders. Often they were greedy men who "collected" dioceses for the sake of the added income. The Cardinal of Lorraine, a powerful French nobleman, was archbishop of Rheims at the age of fourteen. He also had two other archdioceses, seven dioceses, and four wealthy abbeys. In England Cardinal Wolsey was archbishop of York and bishop of three other dioceses. He never set foot in any of his four cathedrals until the day when he was carried into one of them for his funeral.

The clergy with whom laypeople had the most contact were the parish priests, and there were numerous complaints about them. In many localities there were too many of them. In a notorious example, in the German city of Breslau, there were two churches staffed by 236 "altar priests," whose sole duty was celebrating Masses for the dead.

In such churches, where many Masses were celebrated every day at the same time on side altars, many people would run from one Mass to the next to be present at the elevation of the Host. For many the Eucharist had become an object of adoration rather than a sacrament to be celebrated. Sadly too many people came to think of the Mass as the priest's own private prayer rather than a common act of worship.

There were no seminaries to provide priests with proper educational and spiritual formation. So it is not surprising that another common complaint was that many of the priests were poorly trained for their ministry. Things became so bad that one bishop claimed that more than half of his priests could not recite the Ten Commandments and that some of them could not identify the author of the Our Father.

This may have been an exaggeration, but there are other examples. Saint Vincent de Paul, the great French Catholic reformer, used to tell the story about a devout layman who always brought a card containing the words of absolution with him when he went to confession. He would give the priest the card to read because he had discovered that priests sometimes did not know the words. Vincent de Paul also said, "There is nothing so grand as a good priest." He and other Catholic reformers made it a high priority to provide the Church with good and holy priests because he knew how badly they were needed.

We must remember that the Church at this time was suffering but not dead. People still wanted to live as Christ had taught. The saints of the period give ready testimony to that fact. But because the Church allowed itself to be overcome by the culture of the day, it failed to reform itself completely and would soon have to be renewed in a drastic and unwanted way.

 How do you think the Church should respond to the culture of today?

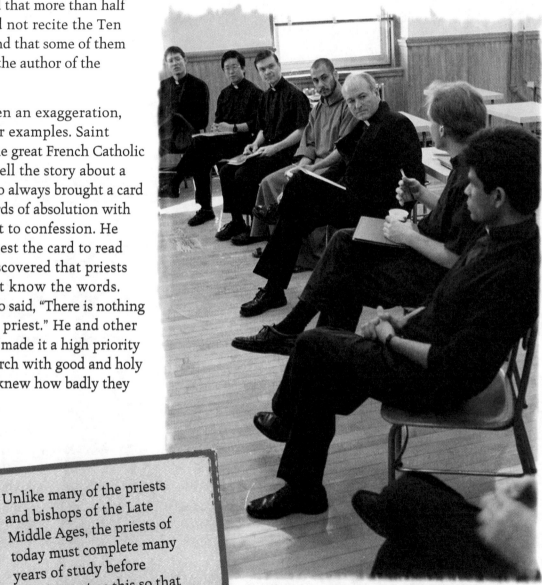

Modern-day seminarians studying theology

CATHOLIC **ID** Unlike many of the priests and bishops of the Late Middle Ages, the priests of today must complete many years of study before ordination. The Church requires this so that they are well prepared to serve God's people.

things to think about

Why is it important that Church leaders have a good education and be spiritually strong people?

Why do you think that many of the holy people of this period in history were not able to help the Church reform itself completely?

WORDS TO REMEMBER

Find and define the following:

Great Schism _____

_____

_____

conciliarism _____

_____

_____

things to share

Someone says to you that the Church is just a human organization like every other. After all, there have been popes and bishops who acted in less than spiritual ways. How would you respond?

How would you explain the Great Schism to one of your friends?

OnLine WITH THE PARISH

Every priest today must spend a number of years in training in a seminary. Find out where the priests in your parish received their seminary training and what it takes to become a priest today.

How did the Avignon papacy lead to a decline in respect for the popes?

1

Explain how the Council of Constance solved one problem but caused another problem?

2

In what ways did the Renaissance have both good and bad effects on the Church?

3

What were the major complaints about bishops in the Late Middle Ages?

4

Who were the Christian humanists, and how did they hope to reform the Church?

5

Life in the Spirit

One of the great saints of this period was Catherine of Siena. The universal Church celebrates her feast on April 29. Through her intercession and prayers, she still serves the Church today. Ask Saint Catherine to pray that you may always have a clear understanding and a great love for Christ's Church.

CHAPTER 7

THE PROTESTANT REFORMATION

A.D. 1517–1603

There is an appointed time
for everything,
and a time for every affair
under the heavens.
Ecclesiastes 3:1

Why do you think it is so hard for people to change and reform their lives? Is change a lifelong process or something that we do once?

Luther's Protest

Although many tried to reform abuses in the Church, some Church leaders opposed reform. They forgot that the Church must constantly reform itself. This is because it is made up of fragile human beings, who often repeat the mistakes of previous generations.

The Church of the Late Middle Ages had survived a long line of crises. On the one hand it had to face internal challenges such as the Avignon papacy, the Great Schism, and conciliarism. On the other hand it had to face a whole new way of looking at the world that was brought about by the Renaissance. But without serious reform within the Church, something had to happen. That something we now call the Protestant Reformation.

Martin Luther,
Cranach the Elder, 1526

The Protestant Reformation is often dated from October 31, 1517. That was the day Martin Luther (1483–1546), a German priest and Augustinian friar, posted his famous Ninety-five Theses on the church door in the little German city of Wittenberg where he lived. These theses were statements protesting abuses, especially the abuse of indulgences.

Indulgences were originally an acceptable way for people to shorten the penances they received in the sacrament of Reconciliation. To gain an indulgence, a person only needed to say certain prayers or perform certain good deeds. By Luther's day, unfortunately, the sale of indulgences had sometimes become a means of raising money for various purposes. And that practice led to abuses.

The particular indulgence to which Luther objected had been approved by Pope Leo X to raise money for the building of St. Peter's Basilica in Rome. In Germany preachers were telling people that they could automatically free their deceased relatives from purgatory simply by obtaining this indulgence for them. Luther was angered by this claim. For him it was too easy an answer, especially

Martin Luther posting his Ninety-five Theses on the door of the Church of All Saints

because he was going through a severe personal and spiritual struggle about his own salvation.

No matter how many prayers Luther said or how many good works he performed, he still feared that God was angry with him and would exclude him from heaven. One day, however, he discovered in the writings of Saint Paul that salvation is a free gift from God to us, not a reward that we earn by our own efforts. Although Luther, a priest, had studied Catholic theology for years, this teaching came as news to him. It gave him the peace of soul that he had been seeking. What Luther did not realize was that this was the traditional teaching of the Catholic Church.

When Luther posted his Ninety-five Theses, he was a Catholic seeking reform within the Church, but events soon made him a rebel. Often when people have a heated argument, they become more and more extreme in their statements and say things that they would not otherwise have said. Something like that happened to Luther between 1517 and 1521. The Ninety-five Theses were an appeal to the local bishop to correct certain abuses of indulgences. When the bishop failed to respond,

Luther appealed to the pope, Leo X. The pope sent Cardinal Cajetan in October 1518 to meet Luther in Germany, but their meeting broke up in anger.

Luther became increasingly radical in his opinions and began to question not only the value of indulgences but also all good works, the authority of the papacy, the sacrifice of the Mass, the ordained priesthood, the monastic life, and most of the sacraments. By November 1518 Luther had also appealed to a Church council. Later he declared that he did not need bishops, popes, or councils and appealed to Scripture as his judge.

In 1520, when Luther refused to give up his views, he was excommunicated by Leo X. In the city of Worms, Emperor Charles V persuaded the legislature (the Diet) of the Holy Roman Empire to declare Luther an outlaw. In his zeal Luther had gone too far. He started out to correct what was wrong and ended up denying some of the most important teachings of the Catholic Church.

Imagine that Luther comes to you with his complaints against the Church. How would you encourage him to remain faithful?

81

Gutenberg Bible, printed in Germany

Print shows how books were made in the late 16th century.

From Luther to Lutheranism

After leaving Worms, Luther returned to Wittenberg, where the local ruler, Frederick the Wise, took him under his protection. Luther lived for another twenty-five years but rarely left his home city again. Thanks to the newly invented printing press, he was able to spread his ideas across Europe more rapidly than any other person before in history.

Luther used his talents to translate the Bible into German and to write books, pamphlets, hymns, and even Christmas carols. Students came to Wittenberg from all over Germany to listen to his lectures and sermons. Luther's convincing message of reform attracted many followers who were tired of abuses in the Church. Very quickly they joined Luther and broke away from the Catholic Church. We call the followers of Martin Luther *Lutherans.*

Fighting broke out between Catholics and Lutherans. In those areas of Germany where the Lutherans won control, major changes occurred in the religious life of the people. The local Catholic parish church became the local Lutheran parish church headed, not by a priest, but by a minister, who was often a married man with a family. The Latin Mass was replaced by a communion service celebrated in German with participation by the congregation. Religious orders were no longer allowed. Lutherans generally recognized only two sacraments, Baptism and the Eucharist, and of course they rejected the authority of the pope and Catholic bishops.

Emperor Charles V remained Luther's sworn enemy. He wanted to wipe out Lutheranism in Germany by force, but he was unable to do so because he was almost constantly at war with the French and the Turks. In 1547 Charles was finally able to bring his army to Germany and defeated the Lutheran princes at the battle of Mühlberg. It was an empty victory, however, for by this time millions of Germans had become Lutherans. Luther had died the year before, but the movement that he had started had taken on a life of its own.

Neither Catholics nor Lutherans could win a complete victory in Germany, and so in 1552 they decided to compromise. This peace settlement was confirmed three years later by the Diet of Augsburg. According to this agreement each of the several hundred German princes and free cities could either remain Catholic or become Lutheran. The ordinary people had no choice except to follow the decision of their rulers or go elsewhere. Most of the rulers in northern and eastern Germany became Lutheran, and most of those in southern and western Germany remained Catholic. This created a religious division that has endured in Germany to the present day.

Zwingli and the Anabaptists

Did all reformers agree with Luther? No. He also faced opposition from fellow Protestants who were more radical than he was. The Swiss city of Zurich experienced its own reformation in the 1520s led by a priest named Huldrych Zwingli (1484–1531), who rejected much more of the Catholic heritage than Luther did. Zwingli abolished such practices as venerating the saints because he said that these activities were not clearly approved in the Bible.

On the one occasion that Luther and Zwingli met, in 1529 in Marburg, they had a heated argument about the Eucharist. Although Luther rejected the sacrifice of the Mass, he believed firmly in the real presence of Christ in the Eucharist. Zwingli insisted that the Eucharist was only bread, a symbol to remind us of the Last Supper.

Luther thought Zwingli was too radical, but there were other Protestants who were even more radical. Some of them appeared in Zurich and criticized Zwingli as a hypocrite. They complained that he was doing things not specifically approved in the Bible, such as collecting tithes (church taxes) and baptizing infants. These extremists were often called *Anabaptists* ("nonbaptizers") because of their opposition to infant Baptism.

Some Anabaptists went too far and even used violence in rejecting the views of others. That is why they were persecuted everywhere by both Catholics and Protestants. The Anabaptists were never very numerous, and often they were uneducated farmers and craftsmen who just wanted to be left alone or to live in their own isolated communities. Some Anabaptist groups, such as the Amish and the Mennonites, eventually emigrated to America, where the Quakers gave them refuge in colonial Pennsylvania.

 What do you know about modern-day Amish and Mennonites in our country?

Modern-day Amish descendants of the Anabaptists

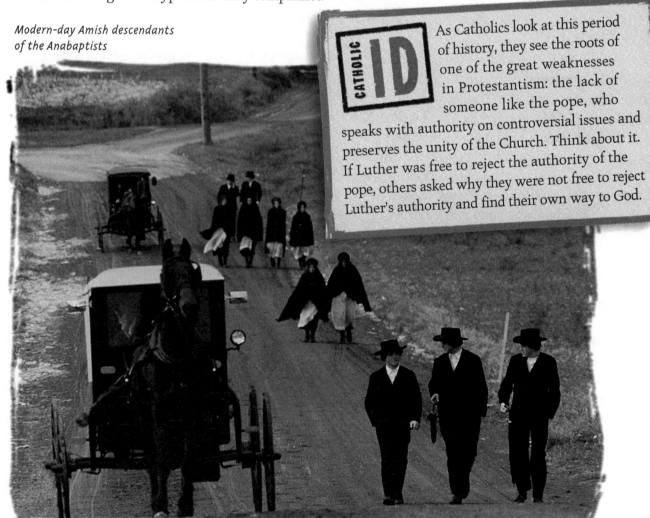

CATHOLIC ID

As Catholics look at this period of history, they see the roots of one of the great weaknesses in Protestantism: the lack of someone like the pope, who speaks with authority on controversial issues and preserves the unity of the Church. Think about it. If Luther was free to reject the authority of the pope, others asked why they were not free to reject Luther's authority and find their own way to God.

John Calvin as a young man, 16th century, Flemish

John Calvin

No one can ignore Luther and his impact on the Protestant Reformation, but there were other reformers. Another Protestant leader was John Calvin (1509–1564). He is not nearly as well known today as Luther, but he is an immensely important figure in Church history. Calvin, who was born in France, was only eight years old when Luther posted his Ninety-five Theses. Unlike Luther, young Calvin was not a particularly religious person, but he experienced a sudden conversion in 1533 and then spent the rest of his life as a zealous Protestant leader.

Unable to live in Catholic France, Calvin finally settled in the French-speaking Swiss city of Geneva, where he made his home for the last twenty-three years of his life. It was not a city that looked kindly on sinners. Everyone was obliged to attend church services on Sunday; drinking, gambling, card playing, and other such vices were strictly forbidden; citizens were encouraged to report one another to the ministers for moral errors. In time Geneva became known as the Calvinist Rome.

Calvin lacked Luther's lively personality; in fact, he was a cold, stern person who was forever in bad health. However, Calvin had a fine mind, some would say a sharper mind than Luther, and his ideas, not his personality, attracted followers. Of course he shared many of Luther's teachings, including his rejection of the Catholic Church and his belief that salvation comes from faith alone and that the Bible was the supreme authority in religious matters.

However, Calvin also differed from Luther in some very important ways. Unlike Luther, Calvin believed in double predestination, a grim doctrine according to which God chooses some people for heaven and some for hell. For Calvin this is God's free decision, and nothing can be done to change it. He also differed from Luther in rejecting the real presence of Christ in the Eucharist. For Calvin, Christ becomes spiritually present to the recipient at the moment of receiving Holy Communion.

The Reformed Religion

Calvin's form of Protestantism had a wider appeal than Luther's. Lutheranism never made many converts outside Germany and Scandinavia. Calvinism, on the other hand, became a great international movement with Geneva as its center. The Calvinists usually called their version of Protestantism the Reformed Religion, and their movement was known by that name throughout much of Europe.

THEN & Now

Our study of Church history helps us to understand modern conflicts such as the troubles in Northern Ireland today. We know that its roots go back to the time of the Reformation. Over the years many Catholics and Protestants have tried to end the violence there. It is important for us to pray that the use of violence to settle conflicts ends everywhere.

In France, Calvin's homeland, the Calvinists were popularly known as Huguenots. Their beliefs were never adopted by the majority of the population, but they were an influential minority and included many nobles and businessmen. In the Netherlands Calvinism became the religion of most of the Dutch. Under the leadership of William of Orange, the Dutch Calvinists won their independence from Catholic Spain and turned their country into one of the wealthiest areas of Europe.

Another place where the Calvinists triumphed was Scotland, which at that time was an independent country. There the key figure was John Knox (1514–1572), a fiery preacher who drove out the Catholic monarch, Mary Stuart, in 1569 and set up the Presbyterian Church of Scotland.

In England success came more slowly to the Calvinists. During the reign of Queen Elizabeth I (1558–1603), most English Calvinists remained members of the Church of England. But they were reluctant members because they thought that this English Protestant Church was too Catholic. They were called Puritans because of their desire to "purify" the Church of England of such Catholic traditions as bishops, vestments, and an elaborate liturgy.

After the death of Elizabeth, however, many English Calvinists left the Church of England to establish their own Presbyterian, Separatist, and Congregationalist churches in defiance of the law. In the 1640s they rose in rebellion under the leadership of Oliver Cromwell, executed King Charles I, and established a short-lived republic. Other English Calvinists sailed across the Atlantic to establish colonies in the New World.

At the same time Scottish Presbyterians were brought to northeastern Ireland and settled on land taken from the Irish Catholics. Calvinism also won many supporters in Germany and in Hungary. In fact, after 1550, Calvinism replaced Lutheranism as the leading edge of the Protestant Reformation.

 As a Catholic why do you think Calvin's teaching about double predestination was wrong?

PROTESTANT REFORMATION

Catholics

Lutherans

Calvinists

Anglicans

0   250   500 Miles
0   250   500 Kilometers

NORWAY
Oslo • Stockholm
SWEDEN
SCOTLAND
Edinburgh • North Sea
IRELAND
Copenhagen
DENMARK
Baltic Sea
ENGLAND
London •
Amsterdam
Wittenberg
POLAND
ATLANTIC OCEAN
Paris •
GERMANY
FRANCE
La Rochelle •
Munich •
Zurich •
SWITZERLAND
HUNGARY
Geneva •
Toulouse •
Adriatic Sea
PORTUGAL Madrid •
ITALY
•Lisbon
Rome •
SPAIN
Mediterranean Sea

85

The English Reformation

In 1521 King Henry VIII of England (1491–1547) reacted strongly when he heard that Luther had written a pamphlet rejecting most of the sacraments. He wrote (or at least claimed to be the author of) a book entitled *Defense of the Seven Sacraments.* The pope was so grateful that he gave Henry the title "Defender of the Faith," which is still used by English monarchs today.

A few years later, however, the Defender of the Faith wanted the pope to release him from his marriage to Queen Catherine of Aragon so that he could marry another woman, Anne Boleyn. Henry had convinced himself that his marriage to Catherine was invalid because she had failed to give him a male heir. Their only child was a daughter, Mary. Henry was equally convinced that if he left the crown to Mary, she would be unable to govern England in such difficult times.

As a Catholic Henry did not believe in divorce. Hence, he asked the pope for an annulment, a declaration that there had never been a true marriage between Catherine and himself. Henry's case, however, rested on very flimsy arguments. Pope Clement VII, a weak and timid man, refused to make a decision; he knew that he could not say yes but was afraid to say no. In 1533, after years of waiting for the pope's answer, Henry took matters into his own hands. He got his handpicked archbishop of Canterbury, Thomas Cranmer (1489–1556), to declare his marriage to Catherine invalid.

When the new pope, Paul III (1534–1549), excommunicated Henry, the king retaliated by having Parliament declare the king supreme head of the Church in England. Unlike Luther and Calvin, however, Henry was not really a Protestant. He did not deny any Catholic doctrine, and he rejected papal authority for personal rather than religious reasons.

Under Henry VIII very little changed in the religion of England except for the break with Rome. Mass was still offered in Latin; the sacraments were still celebrated; the rhythm of parish life was not interrupted. That may explain why so few people resisted Henry's actions. Of all the bishops in England, only one had the courage to challenge the king, John Fisher, bishop of Rochester. Among the laity the leading opponent of Henry was Thomas More, the former lord chancellor. Both men paid a high price for their courage; the king executed them within weeks of each other in 1535.

*Film still from **A Man for All Seasons**, 1966, Paul Scofield (right) as Thomas More; Robert Shaw as Henry VIII*

Mary Tudor, Antonio, 16th century

Mary and Elizabeth I

After the death of Edward VI, a conservative reaction brought to the throne Henry's Catholic daughter Mary Tudor. Mary wanted to restore Catholicism in England, but unfortunately she tried to do it largely by force. In her brief reign (1553–1558), she executed 273 Protestants, including Thomas Cranmer. She has been known ever since in English history as "Bloody Mary."

Mary died without an heir, leaving the crown to her half sister Elizabeth, who was to reign for forty-five years. A strong ruler and skilled politician, Elizabeth was a Protestant who wanted religious peace through political compromise. Like her father, Henry VIII, she had Parliament declare her supreme governor of the Church of England. Then she set about fashioning a middle-of-the-road Protestant Church that she hoped would please everybody. The doctrine of this new church was solidly Protestant. However, Elizabeth left intact the Catholic form of church government with archbishops and bishops.

 Was it easy for John Fisher or Thomas More to stand up to the king? Discuss your ideas.

When Henry VIII died in 1547, England was still basically a Catholic country. However, Edward VI, Henry's son, was only a child when he was crowned, and he and his advisors were devout Protestants. It was during the short reign of this boy king (1547–1553) that the Protestant Reformation was really introduced into England. The key figure in bringing about this change was Thomas Cranmer, the archbishop of Canterbury, who now had a free hand to make the doctrinal and liturgical changes that he dared not attempt while Henry was alive.

Under Cranmer's leadership the Mass was now replaced with a communion service in English. Cranmer composed a beautiful liturgy based on the Book of Common Prayer, which he compiled. However, it was a liturgy that no Catholic could accept because it rejected both the sacrifice of the Mass and the belief in the real presence of Christ in the Eucharist.

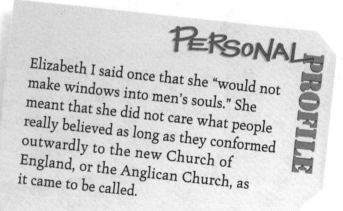

PERSONAL PROFILE

Elizabeth I said once that she "would not make windows into men's souls." She meant that she did not care what people really believed as long as they conformed outwardly to the new Church of England, or the Anglican Church, as it came to be called.

things to think about

Why do Catholics think that the reformers of this period went too far in their efforts?

What evidence do we have of Calvin's powerful influence in the United States today?

things to share

Someone says that all Christians are really the same. Knowing about the Protestant Reformation, what would you say?

Some of the Protestant reformers said that the Eucharist is only a symbol, not the Body and Blood of Christ. As a Catholic how would you respond?

WORDS TO REMEMBER

Find and define the following:

Lutherans _____
_____
_____

Anabaptists _____
_____
_____

OnLine

WITH THE PARISH

Find out how many Protestant communities are located within the boundaries of your Catholic parish. See whether or not you can trace the history of each of these Protestant Churches back to one of the Protestant leaders mentioned in this chapter.

Why was Martin Luther angry about the way that indulgences were being sold in the Church of his day?

1

How did the peace settlement confirmed by the Diet of Augsburg in 1555 end the fighting between Lutherans and Catholics in Germany?

2

Why were both Protestants and Catholics alarmed by the Anabaptists?

3

How did the teachings of John Calvin differ from those of Martin Luther?

4

How did Queen Elizabeth I try to organize a middle-of-the-road Protestant Church in England?

5

Life in the Spirit

Catholics revere men such as Thomas More and John Fisher, who died as martyrs for their Catholic faith. Protestants show a similar reverence for their martyrs, such as Thomas Cranmer. Do you think it is possible and appropriate for a Catholic also to respect Protestant martyrs? Can a Catholic do this without being disloyal to his or her own faith?

CHAPTER 8

THE COUNTER-REFORMATION
A.D. 1545–1648

If you are wise, then know that you have
been created for the glory of God. . . .
This is the treasure of your heart.

Saint Robert Bellarmine

What do you do when faced with a crisis?
Where do you go for advice? How do you decide
on a plan of action to deal with the crisis?

The Council of Trent

General councils are rare events in the history of the Catholic Church. Usually they have been held only during times of crisis. The Protestant Reformation was one of the greatest crises the Church ever faced, and the council that was summoned to deal with that crisis was the Council of Trent. This council had such a powerful effect on the Church that its influence lasted well into the twentieth century.

The Protestant Reformation began in 1517, but the Council of Trent did not meet until 1545. Why was there such a long delay? There were several reasons. The popes feared that a general council would lead to a revival of conciliarism (the theory that the authority of a general council is superior even to that of the pope). Emperor Charles V, the ruler of Germany, was eager to have a council, but

the pope was afraid that he would try to control it and use it for his own purposes. Even the meeting place was a matter of dispute. Charles wanted the council to meet in Germany; the pope wanted it to meet in Rome. The compromise choice was Trent, a little city high in the Alps on the border between Germany and Italy.

It took Pope Paul III eight years to bring together the Council of Trent in 1545. The council met three times over the next eighteen years and produced more decrees than all eighteen general councils that had preceded it. The number of bishops in attendance was not large, usually no more than a hundred, and northern Europe was hardly represented at all. Some Protestant representatives appeared at the second session in 1551 but quickly left.

92

Achievements of Trent

The emperor wanted the council to concentrate on the elimination of abuses; the pope wanted the council to emphasize the explanation of Catholic doctrine. The council decided to do both. It never mentioned Luther or Calvin by name, and it did not persuade the Protestants to return to the Catholic Church. But it explained in clear and direct language the teachings of the Church on many vital issues, such as the means of salvation, the nature of the Mass and the other sacraments, purgatory, indulgences, papal authority, and the veneration of the saints. No one could any longer wonder what the official teaching of the Church was on any important matter.

The Council of Trent also devoted much attention to the elimination of abuses in the Church. It issued rules to eliminate the sale of indulgences and to improve the quality of the bishops and priests. King Philip II of Spain complained that the council increased the authority of the pope at the expense of the bishops. King Philip's criticism was not altogether fair, however. Although the pope's authority was increased, so was that of the bishops. They were to be the workhorses in reforming the Church. The council ordered the bishops to live in their dioceses, preach regularly, visit every parish each year, watch over monasteries and convents, supervise hospitals and charitable institutions, and set a personal example of good Christian conduct.

The Council of Trent also gave careful attention to the reform of the parish clergy. Its most important practical reform was the decree ordering every bishop to establish a seminary in his diocese. The new kind of priest who emerged from these seminaries helped to restore respect for the priesthood and to lead to a spiritual revival where it was most needed—in the local parishes throughout the Catholic world. Through the Council of Trent, the Church found an important way to answer, or counter, the crisis begun by the Protestant Reformation. That is why we call this period the *Counter-Reformation.*

Trent and the Papacy

Without the determination of Pope Paul III, the Council of Trent would never have met. Paul III, who is generally considered the first of the Counter-Reformation popes, spent eight long years clearing away the obstacles in the council's path. He himself began his career in Rome in the bad old days of Pope Alexander VI. In fact Paul III had been made a cardinal because Alexander VI was in love with Paul's sister. By the time that Paul III was elected pope in 1534, he had undergone a positive spiritual reformation in his own life, and as pope he tried to communicate the results of that reformation to the rest of the Church.

One of Paul III's first acts was to appoint a committee to tell him what was wrong in the Church. The committee reported bluntly that many of the abuses came from the misdeeds of previous popes. Paul III began to correct those abuses. Because he could not accomplish this huge task by himself, he surrounded himself with reform-minded advisors, many of whom he made cardinals. He also had the good judgment to approve a new religious order that was to play a major role in the reform of the Church. That order was the Society of Jesus, or the Jesuits.

Paul III worked closely with the Council of Trent, but he had to suspend it in 1547 because of other pressures. His successor, Pope Julius III (1550–1555), called the council back into session and encouraged its work. The next pope, Marcellus II, would almost certainly have done the same, but he died a few weeks after his election. Both Julius and Marcellus had served as legates (papal delegates) to the council and knew at first hand the wonderful contribution that it was making to the reform of the Church.

However, the next pope, Paul IV (1555–1559), very nearly wrecked the Counter-Reformation. Almost eighty years old when he was elected, Paul IV was like a self-appointed prophet. He insisted that he could reform the Church by himself. He refused to reconvene the Council of Trent, nearly dissolved the Jesuits, and even suspected some of the cardinals of being secret Protestants. He was ruthless in rooting out corruption in Rome itself, but the task of reforming the whole Church was too big for one man to accomplish by himself.

His successor, Pius IV (1559–1565), was a more moderate man who did the Church an immense service by reassembling the Council of Trent in 1562, after a lapse of ten years. He then patiently brought the council to a successful conclusion the following year and approved its decrees. The bishops at Trent did not have time to accomplish everything that they wished, and so they left much unfinished business in the hands of the papacy. Hence the first three popes after the council—the first *Tridentine* popes, as they are called because the word means "having to do with the Council of Trent"—had the huge responsibility of putting its reforms into practice.

Papal document issued by Pope Pius IV in 1560 to recall the Council of Trent

94

Pope Pius V

Looking up at the dome of St. Peter's Basilica

CATHOLIC ID

When Sixtus V became pope, the dome of St. Peter's Basilica was still unfinished. He asked the architects how long it would take to complete it. They said, "Ten years." He threatened to hang them if the dome was not finished sooner. The architects completed their work in twenty-two months. Sixtus V was a pope who got things done!

The First Tridentine Popes

The first Tridentine pope was Pius V (1566–1572), a saintly Dominican friar who is one of the few modern popes to be canonized. He furthered the work of reform by publishing a catechism that summarized the teachings of the Council of Trent. He also issued a revised missal, the liturgical book used in the celebration of Mass.

His successor was Gregory XIII (1572–1585), who took a deep interest in Catholic education and in the foreign missions. He also started the papal diplomatic corps by dispatching ambassadors (called nuncios) to the Catholic capitals of Europe. He is best remembered today for setting up the modern calendar that every country in the world uses today.

The third Tridentine pope was Sixtus V (1585–1590). He crowded a lifetime of work into a pontificate of only five years. He rebuilt much of Rome and gave the papacy an effective administrative system. Thanks to the leadership of all these Tridentine popes, by 1600 the reforms of the Council of Trent were beginning to be felt throughout the Church.

 Why do you think the Counter-Reformation was such an important time for the Church?

The Society of Jesus

The most famous of the new religious communities was the Society of Jesus. It was founded by Saint Ignatius of Loyola (1491–1556) in 1534. Ignatius was a former Spanish soldier who experienced a religious conversion as he was recovering from a war wound. His new religious order, which he called a society, reflected his own military background, for it was built around strict obedience to superiors. Ignatius also required a long period of apprenticeship and education for his followers, who were soon called Jesuits. He made some daring innovations: Jesuits did not wear a distinctive habit, and they were not required to pray together in common as members of other religious orders did. "We are not monks.... The world is our house," said Jerome Nadal, one of the first Jesuits.

The Jesuits quickly gained a reputation as some of the finest teachers in Europe, and their schools were highly regarded. The Jesuits also became famous as missionaries both to the Protestant areas of Europe and overseas in North and South America and the Far East. The growth of their numbers was astounding. Ignatius began with six recruits in 1534; at the time of his death in 1556, there were a thousand Jesuits; by 1600 there were thirteen thousand.

Many Jesuits were outstanding individuals who have since been canonized. Saint Francis Xavier (1506–1552), one of the original Jesuits, became known as the apostle of the Indies because of his missionary work in India and Japan. Saint Isaac Jogues (1607–1646) and Saint Jean de Brébeuf (1593–1649) both died as martyrs while serving as missionaries in North America.

Saint Edmund Campion (1540–1581) suffered a martyr's death in England while trying to preserve the Catholic faith there. Saint Peter Canisius (1521–1597) is known as the second apostle of Germany because of his success in reconverting many Protestants to Catholicism. Saint Robert Bellarmine (1542–1621) was one of the great theologians of the day. Even the great-grandson of the sinful Pope Alexander VI, Saint Francis Borgia (1510–1572), showed the world that grace can overcome heredity.

Saint Robert Bellarmine

Saint Angela Merici

Saint Ignatius of Loyola

Other New Orders

Among the Franciscans there was a movement to return to the strict observance of the vow of poverty. These friars eventually formed a new order known as the Capuchins. Faithful to the spirit of Saint Francis, they worked among the poor and the uneducated. For that reason their labors were not as well recorded as those of the Jesuits, but there can be no doubt that they made a major contribution to the Church.

Saint Vincent de Paul (1581–1660) was one of the giants of the Counter-Reformation in France. He founded a new order, the Congregation of the Mission, to bring the gospel to the neglected peasants in the rural areas of France. His priests (popularly known today in the United States as Vincentians) also staffed seminaries.

In Spain Saint Teresa of Ávila (1515–1582), one of the greatest spiritual writers of all time, led the reform of the Carmelite Order. She was a spirited woman of aristocratic background who always said what was on her mind. Saint Teresa's Carmelite nuns were *cloistered religious*. That is, they never left the convent and devoted themselves entirely to a life of prayer. This was the traditional form of religious life for women.

A new kind of woman religious appeared at this time, however, nuns and sisters whose vocation took them out into the world to work as teachers and nurses. The pioneer in this movement was Saint Angela Merici (1474–1540), whom we have already met. With a few companions she began to teach poor girls in 1535. In 1565 this little group evolved into the Order of Saint Ursula, the oldest and largest teaching order of women in the Church.

Another woman with similar intentions was Saint Jane Frances de Chantal (1572–1641). She, too, wished to establish an order of unenclosed nuns who would work in the world. However, opposition to this novel idea was too strong, and her Order of the Visitation became a traditional cloistered order.

Another Frenchwoman, Saint Louise de Marillac (1591–1660), met with more success. Together with Saint Vincent de Paul, she founded the Daughters of Charity around 1633. The order grew rapidly in France, working among the poor as schoolteachers and nurses. Many of the Daughters of Charity came from the poor. That, too, was an innovation because most convents required a large dowry (entrance fee) that poor young women often could not afford to pay.

 *Choose one of the new religious orders of the Counter-Reformation. Tell how it responded to the needs of the Church.*

Saint Vincent de Paul and the Daughters of Charity, Ansiaux, 19th century

THEN & Now

Many of the religious communities that were important during the Counter-Reformation are still important today. Following the request of the Church, these groups have reformed themselves according to the spirit of the men and women who founded them. Such communities are a true and ever vital gift to the Church on its pilgrim way.

Queen Elizabeth I, Hilliard, late 16th century

Elizabeth I and the Church

One of the most fascinating chapters in the history of the Counter-Reformation is the story of the Catholic Church in England under Queen Elizabeth I (1558–1603). In the 1560s it seemed almost certain that the Catholic Church would disappear in England. Elizabeth wanted to eliminate it, but she did not want to make Catholic martyrs as her half sister Mary ("Bloody Mary") had made Protestant martyrs. Instead she came up with a clever way to get rid of the Catholic Church in England quietly and peacefully.

Elizabeth had a threefold plan. First, she arrested the Catholic bishops, which meant that there would be no more ordinations of future priests. Second, she ordered the existing clergy to join the new Protestant Church of England, which most of them did. Third, she threatened to tax laypeople if they did not attend Protestant Church services every Sunday.

It was a shrewd plan, and it almost worked. The Catholic Church cannot survive long anywhere without the Eucharist, and the Eucharist cannot be celebrated without priests. Elizabeth knew that, and so she just sat back and waited for the last Catholic priests in England to die. Then the Catholic Church itself would die out.

The Douai Priests

One person especially deserves credit for spoiling Elizabeth's plan and saving the Catholic Church in England from extinction. His name was William Allen (1532–1594). He was an English Catholic priest who refused to accept Elizabeth's new Protestant Church. He left England and settled across the Channel in the little city of Douai in what is now Belgium. There he started a seminary to train English priests. Young Catholic men in England heard about Douai and went there to study for the priesthood. Allen's original plan was to have a supply of Catholic priests ready when Elizabeth died and England once again became a Catholic country. However, Elizabeth was in no hurry to die, and Allen said, "We cannot wait for better times; we must create them."

Allen started to send back to England the newly ordained priests of Douai. They could not practice their ministry publicly, but they traveled in disguise from one Catholic household to the next. There they secretly celebrated Mass, heard confessions,

Cardinal William Allen, engraving,
Cochran, late 16th century

preached, and anointed the sick. An underground Catholic Church sprang up centered in the manor houses of the Catholic landowners. Many of these houses had hiding places where priests could take refuge if there was a raid by the police.

When Elizabeth saw what was happening, she was furious. It ruined her plans to strangle the Catholic Church in England quietly. She began to persecute Catholics, especially the missionary priests. It soon became high treason merely to be a Catholic priest in England. Priests who were seized were executed in the most grisly way possible, by being "hung, drawn and quartered." That is, they were hung from a gallows but then cut down while still alive and hacked to pieces by the public executioner. The first of the Douai priests to suffer this fate was Saint Cuthbert Mayne (1544–1577), who was executed in November 1577.

The blood of martyrs is the seed of the Church, however. The more priests Elizabeth executed, the more young men applied for admission to Douai and the other English seminaries that were founded on the Continent. In the last thirty years of Elizabeth's reign, Douai alone ordained 440 diocesan priests, and 98 died as martyrs. It is no wonder that historians speak of the Elizabethan era as the golden age of the Catholic priesthood. It was these priests (and the laypeople who sheltered them) who kept alive the Catholic faith under the most difficult circumstances.

The way in which the popes of this period dealt with England is controversial. Pope Pius V excommunicated Elizabeth I and ordered English Catholics not to recognize her as their legitimate ruler. This gave the queen the excuse to say that Catholics could not be loyal subjects and to persecute them as traitors. Pope Gregory XIII went even further and organized two unsuccessful invasions of England.

When the missionary priests were arrested, they were asked the "bloody question": In the event of an invasion of England, whom would you support, the pope or the queen? Many priests refused to answer the question because they wanted to be loyal to both their Church and their country. Neither the pope nor the queen made it easy for them to be both faithful Catholics and faithful Englishmen. These loyal Catholics were the real heroes of the Catholic Church in England under Queen Elizabeth I.

You are a Catholic in the England of Elizabeth I. Send a report to Rome about the success of Douai in outwitting Elizabeth.

things to think about

Why do you think religious orders played such an important part in the reform of the Church?

In England under Queen Elizabeth I, Catholics had a difficult time trying to be both loyal Catholics and loyal English subjects. Do Americans ever face such a problem today? If so, why?

things to share

Using as few words as possible, tell why the Council of Trent was one of the most important events in the history of the Catholic Church.

Why was the Counter-Reformation so important?

WORDS TO REMEMBER

Find and define the following:

Counter-Reformation _____
_____
_____

Tridentine _____
_____
_____

OnLine
WITH THE PARISH

Women religious—nuns and sisters—have made an enormous contribution to the Catholic Church in the United States. Find out what communities of women religious have been associated with your parish. See whether you can find out when and where these religious communities originated and what kind of works their members do today.

Why did Pope Paul III have great difficulty in convening the Council of Trent?

1

How did the first three Tridentine popes put into practice the reforms of the council?

2

The early history of the Society of Jesus is an amazing story. Why?

3

What contribution did women religious make to the Counter-Reformation?

4

Life in the Spirit

The followers of Saint Ignatius of Loyola, the Jesuits, are all over the world. One of them, the English priest and poet Gerard Manley Hopkins (1844–1889), wrote: "The world is charged with the grandeur of God." Think about these words. What do they say to you?

Why is the reign of Queen Elizabeth I considered the golden age of the Catholic priesthood in England?

5

BETWEEN
REFORMATION AND
REVOLUTION
A.D. 1648–1789

Go, therefore, and
make disciples of all nations.
Matthew 28:19

What does it mean to be truly free?
How do you feel when someone
unjustly limits your freedom?

The Great Age of Kings

Sometimes we can lose our freedom without even realizing it. It just slips away, slowly but surely. In many ways the same thing can be said about the Church in Europe during the period from 1648 to 1789. On the surface it appears that nothing much happened during this time to limit the Church's freedom. But nothing could be further from the truth.

Between 1618 and 1648, a period known as the Thirty Years' War, Protestants and Catholics were still in conflict. In 1648 the Treaties of Westphalia brought an end to the wars of religion, leaving Europe divided between Protestant and Catholic states. The following 150 years were the great age of kings in Europe. A new kind of monarch appeared: the absolute monarch. These rulers had virtually unlimited power over their subjects. They tried to control every aspect of their people's lives, including their religion.

In the Catholic countries of Europe, the absolute monarchs posed a grave threat to the freedom of the Church. That may seem like a strange comment to make because these rulers showered all kinds of favors on the Church. They made the Catholic Church the "established" Church in their kingdoms, which meant that only Catholics could worship publicly. Protestants even had to be buried in Catholic cemeteries with Catholic ceremonies.

The parish priests were civil officials in charge of such vital statistics as the registration of births, marriages, and deaths. Government announcements were usually made by the priest from the pulpit at Sunday Mass. All schools and charitable institutions were under the control of the Church. The clergy were great landowners and paid no taxes; indeed, they collected their own tax, which was called a *tithe*. A tithe usually involved giving ten percent of one's income to the Church.

However, the Catholic Church paid a heavy price for being the established Church. That price was government control. The absolute monarchs in Catholic countries tried to dominate the Church much as Henry VIII had dominated the Church in England in his day. Of course none of them ever formally rejected the authority of the pope as Henry did, but they tried to whittle down his power and that of the bishops as much as they could. Because they usually controlled the appointment of bishops and abbots, they selected candidates who would be obedient to them. Does this sound familiar? It should. It was simply another version of caesaropapism, the age-old desire of *caesar* to be *papa*, a problem that goes back to Constantine in the fourth century.

Two examples will illustrate the harm that the Church suffered in these years, not from Protestants or unbelievers, but from monarchs who prided themselves on being sincere Catholics. In France, the leading Catholic country in the world, King Louis XIV (who reigned from 1643 to 1715) engaged in a long tug-of-war with the pope over the appointment of bishops. In order to put pressure on the pope, in 1682 the king assembled the French bishops and had them sign a declaration called the Gallican Articles that severely crippled the pope's authority in France. It was a peculiarly French form of caesaropapism that was called *Gallicanism* (from the Latin word for "French").

In Austria, the second most important Catholic country, Emperor Joseph II (who reigned from 1780 to 1790) was even more aggressive than Louis XIV in his interference in Church affairs. *Josephinism,* as his form of caesaropapism was called, included taxing the clergy, abolishing hundreds of monasteries, establishing state-run seminaries, and even regulating the number of candles to be used at Mass! Pope Pius VI was so alarmed at Joseph's activities that he traveled to Vienna in 1782 to plead with him personally to stop. The emperor received the pope courteously but paid no attention to his complaints.

In other Catholic countries the situation was similar. Rulers exercised more control over the Church. Not all of their interference was bad. But the one thing that these rulers would not give the Church was the freedom to run its own affairs.

Knowing about the history of the Church to this point, do you think the American form of government deals well with religion in everyday life?

How does this image symbolize the tensions of this period?

A Challenge for Catholics

After 1648 in the Protestant countries of Europe, the established Protestant Churches enjoyed the same exclusive privileges that the Catholic Church had in Catholic countries. In some Protestant countries, Catholicism completely died out. In Sweden and northeastern Germany, for example, a person could travel for hundreds of miles without ever coming across a Catholic church.

In some Protestant countries, however, organized Catholic life continued to exist, often under very difficult circumstances. In Switzerland and the Dutch Netherlands, there were substantial Catholic minorities and flourishing Catholic communities. In the highlands of Scotland, an overwhelmingly Protestant country, small pockets of Gaelic-speaking Scottish Catholics clung to their faith.

We have already mentioned that heroic English missionary priests kept the faith alive in their homeland despite the savage penalties inflicted on them by Queen Elizabeth I. Later a prominent Catholic layman, George Calvert (1579–1632), the first Lord Baltimore, received permission from King Charles I to establish a colony in the New World for persecuted English Catholics.

In 1634 a group sailed across the Atlantic in two tiny ships, the *Ark* and the *Dove,* to establish the colony of Maryland (named in honor of the king's wife). This happened only fourteen years after another group of persecuted Englishmen and Englishwomen, the Pilgrims, had crossed the Atlantic on the *Mayflower.*

The descendants of the Pilgrims in Puritan Massachusetts were unwilling to allow freedom of worship to other Christians. But in Maryland, even though Catholics were always a minority, they worked for religious toleration for all Christians in the colony. Unfortunately Maryland's Protestant majority later deprived the Catholic minority of religious freedom.

But things were different in Pennsylvania. That colony was founded in 1681 by William Penn as a place of refuge for his fellow Quakers, who were persecuted in England as dangerous religious radicals. The Quakers were one of the few religious groups of that day who not only wanted religious freedom for themselves but also were willing to give it to others. The Amish and Mennonites, who were Anabaptists, found a place of refuge in Quaker Pennsylvania. So did Catholics.

CATHOLIC ID Saint Joseph's Church in Philadelphia dates from 1733. On the front of the building is a plaque reminding visitors that in 1733 this church was the only place in the whole English-speaking world (except for chapels in the London embassies of Catholic countries) where it was legal to celebrate Mass.

The Irish Catholics

Perhaps the most remarkable example of Catholic survival in Protestant Europe is what happened in Ireland. The majority of the Irish people remained Catholic, but their country was completely taken over by the English in the seventeenth century. Land was the basis of political power and wealth at this time. For that reason the English conquerors took possession of almost all the land in Ireland. The Irish Catholics were now tenants on land that they had once owned.

Ruins of an early Irish Catholic church

English policy in Ireland was not to exterminate the Irish Catholics but to keep them in a permanent state of dependence. To achieve this goal, the English established the infamous Penal Laws, which were designed to deprive the Irish Catholics of land, education, and political power. As a final insult the Irish were forced to give financial support to a foreign Protestant Church that they despised while their own Catholic faith was outlawed.

Like English Catholics under Queen Elizabeth I, the Irish Catholics formed an underground Church to keep their faith alive. Their priests, who were trained in seminaries on the continent of Europe, traveled in disguise throughout the country, often celebrating Mass at outdoor altars. The altars had to be outdoors because the Catholics were forbidden to build their own churches. Sometimes, when Mass was celebrated in private homes, the people would gather in a separate room from the priest. That way, if the priest was later arrested, they might be able to save his life by swearing that they had not seen him celebrate Mass.

Toward the end of the eighteenth century, the persecution of Catholics had pretty well ended in Protestant countries (as had the persecution of Protestants in Catholic countries). At least in England, Ireland, Scotland, and the new United States of America, Catholics now enjoyed a degree of religious toleration. They did not have full civil rights and often suffered from discrimination, but they were truly better off than they had been a century earlier.

Now that you know your ancestors in faith did not enjoy their full civil rights, how do you feel about those who struggle for their civil rights today?

Bartolomé de Las Casas, Spanish engraving, 18th century

An Exciting Age

Some people think that Catholicism is a European religion. The word *catholic,* however, means just the opposite. It means that Catholicism is universal, for people of all races, languages, and nationalities.

The Catholic faith originated, not in Europe, but in the Greco-Roman world that included Europe, Asia, and North Africa. We have already seen that in the early Church some of the most vigorous centers of Christianity were to be found in North Africa and Asia. However, the rise of Islam in the seventh century completely changed the geography of Christianity. The Christian world was reduced primarily to the continent of Europe, and that was still true at the time of the Reformation.

During the lifetime of Luther, however, European navigators discovered North and South America and sailed around the continent of Africa to open a direct route to India and the Far East. What an exciting age this must have been! For the first time Europe was brought into contact with the rest of the world. These discoveries had an enormous impact on the Church, too. The reason? Where the discoverer first went, the missionary soon followed.

In 1492 Columbus discovered America, and the Portuguese were already inching their way down the west coast of Africa. In 1493 Pope Alexander VI drew an imaginary line dividing these new discoveries between Spain and Portugal. Everything west of the line went to Spain; everything east of the line went to Portugal. That is why Brazil today is a Portuguese-speaking country.

Missionaries accompanied Columbus on his second expedition in 1493 and began the evangelization of the native peoples of the Americas. This was largely the work of Franciscan and Dominican friars. They have been criticized for failing to give their converts sufficient instruction before Baptism and for failing to recognize what was good in the native religions. Whether or not this criticism was true, we know that by 1600 there were millions of Christians in Latin America.

Both the Spanish crown and the pope forbade the enslavement of the Indians, but it was difficult to enforce such laws thousands of miles away in Latin America. Spanish missionaries deserve credit for their efforts to prevent enslavement. Antonio Montesino (1468–1530) and Bartolomé de Las Casas (1474–1566), both Dominican friars, have sometimes been called the first modern civil rights leaders because of their defense of the Indians.

The Native Americans suffered terribly from their contact with Europeans. They had no immunity to European diseases and died by the millions. To replace them as laborers in the mines and plantations, the Spanish and Portuguese imported millions of slaves from Africa.

Many Parts of the World

Catholic missionaries also accompanied Portuguese expeditions to the Far East. Here the outstanding figure was Saint Francis Xavier (1506–1552), who arrived in India in 1542. From there he traveled to Indonesia and then, in 1549, to Japan. He died on his way to China. In India Francis Xavier baptized thousands of people with a minimum of religious instruction. In Japan he proceeded more slowly, trying to understand the culture and religion of the Japanese before he presented the Christian religion to them.

Christianity reached many other parts of the world as well. The French established missions to the Indians in Canada and much of the American Midwest. Japanese Catholics brought the faith to Vietnam, where French missionaries assisted them. The Spanish planted the seeds of faith in the Philippines, which today is the only predominantly Catholic country in Asia. Portuguese and French missionaries were active in Africa, but their efforts were cut short by the slave trade. The real evangelization of Africa did not take place until the nineteenth century.

In 1622 the pope established the Congregation for the Propagation of the Faith (now called the Congregation for the Evangelization of Peoples) to supervise the worldwide activities of Catholic missionaries. This was a recognition that the Catholic Church had now spread far beyond Europe and could claim to be more truly "catholic" than at any time since the first few centuries of Christianity.

What advice would you give to modern-day missionaries in dealing with peoples of different cultures?

After the success of early missionaries in Japan, the government turned hostile to Christianity. In 1597 twenty-six Catholic missionaries and converts were crucified in Nagasaki. It was the beginning of a cruel persecution. By 1636 thirty-five thousand Christians were killed, and Japan soon cut itself off from all contact with the outside world until the middle of the nineteenth century.

Saint Francis Xavier: Apostle of the Indies,
French lithograph, 19th century

The Scientific Revolution

While the European explorers were discovering other parts of the world, in Europe itself other people were raising disturbing questions about life. A quiet revolution was taking place in the way that people viewed the world around them. They were becoming more curious, more critical, more demanding of proofs for the things they believed. New tools and instruments such as the telescope and the microscope made possible huge leaps in human knowledge. This new way of looking at the world is called the *scientific revolution,* and it was as important as any political revolution in history.

When did all this start? The year 1642 is a good place to begin an account of the scientific revolution. That was the year in which Galileo died and Newton was born. They were the two great giants in this revolution of the mind. Galileo (1564–1642) proved that Earth revolves around the Sun, and not the other way around, as was generally believed. Sir Isaac Newton (1642–1727) discovered the law of universal gravitation.

Scholars made important contributions in many other fields as well. William Harvey (1578–1657), an English physician, discovered the circulation of blood, and geologists showed from their study of rocks that Earth was much older than had been supposed. History was still another field that experienced revolutionary changes as historians learned to weigh evidence carefully and to separate fact from legend.

How did all these things affect the Church? Most of the scholars and scientists who were responsible for the scientific revolution had no intention of calling into question any Christian doctrines. But their discoveries often raised puzzling questions for Christians. The most famous example is that of Galileo, who was condemned by the Church for saying that Earth revolves around the Sun. Church authorities in Rome said that Galileo must be wrong because his theory appeared to contradict what was written in the Bible. Under pressure Galileo signed a statement taking back his own discovery.

Geologists also raised uncomfortable questions. They proved that Earth was millions of years old, much older than biblical evidence would seem to indicate. A French priest, Richard Simon (1638–1712), wrote a book in which he tried to show that it is not necessary to interpret everything in the Bible literally and that people should look to it for religious truths, not scientific facts. Simon was condemned by bishops and theologians for lack of faith. They much preferred the views of someone who claimed to have figured out the exact day that God created the world.

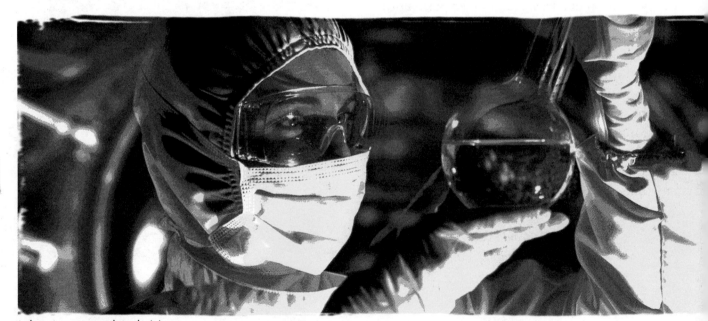

Laboratory research technician

These disagreements between scientists and theologians opened a gap and caused mistrust between science and religion that still lingers with some people even three centuries later. Much of the initial fault lies with the theologians who stubbornly refused to consider the new facts discovered by the scientists. It was a mistake that Saint Thomas Aquinas would not have made. He was never afraid of new knowledge because he was convinced that truth cannot contradict truth.

The Enlightenment

"The Church has nothing to fear from the progress of science," Pope Pius XI said. But in the eighteenth century, a movement to popularize the new science took on a strongly antireligious tone. The proponents of this movement called it the *Enlightenment* because they saw themselves bringing the light of science to a world sunk in the darkness of religious superstition. The Enlightenment affected all of Europe and America, too, but its center was France. There it produced clever and witty writers such as Voltaire, whose barbs were often directed at the Church.

These writers were not Christians, but neither were they atheists. Most of them said that their religion was *Deism*. Deists did not believe in the Bible or divine revelation. But they said that they knew that there was a supreme Being on the basis of reason alone. However, the God of the Deists had no interest whatsoever in the world that he had created or in any creature in it. The Deists liked to speak of God as the Great Architect of the universe. They would never have dreamed of addressing him in prayer as Our Father.

The Enlightenment and the Deism that grew out of it represented a new challenge for the Church. At the time of the Reformation, Christians quarreled over the identity of the true Christian Church. Now the Deists and others influenced by the Enlightenment rejected Christianity itself in favor of a religion based solely on reason and science. They claimed that with this new religion they could make their own paradise on earth.

 Are you aware of any conflicts between religion and science today? What are they?

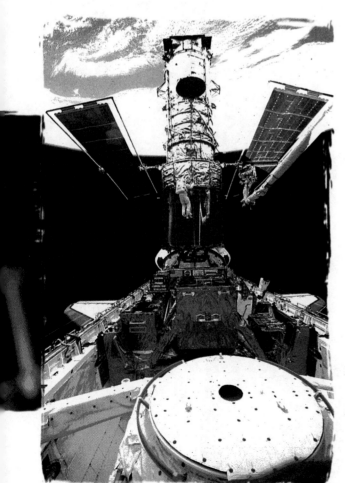

Hubble space telescope with backdrop of Australia

PUTTING IT TOGETHER

things to think about

Why do you think the Church should be free to run its own affairs in every country of the world?

Why does it seem that periods of persecution make the Church grow stronger?

things to share

If someone tells you that everything the Church did in bringing faith to the New World was wrong, what would you say?

How would you as a Catholic compare your idea of God with a Deist's idea of God?

WORDS TO REMEMBER

Find and define the following:

Enlightenment _____
_____
_____

Gallicanism _____
_____
_____

OnLine WITH THE PARISH

Many parishes sponsor adult education programs featuring modern Catholic interpretations of the Bible. See whether such a program is offered in your parish. Perhaps you and your group can offer prayerful support to your fellow parishioners who are studying God's word.

What special privileges did the Catholic Church enjoy in the Catholic countries of Europe in the eighteenth century?

1

What did the Irish Catholics do to preserve their faith under persecution?

2

Why can we compare Father Bartolomé de Las Casas to the civil rights leaders of our own day?

3

How did the scientific revolution change the way that people looked at the world around them?

4

What was the Deists' attitude toward God and the Catholic Church?

5

Life
in the Spirit

We learn from science *how* the world was created and how human beings first made their appearance on earth. We learn from the Bible *why* God created the world and why he created men and women. Take a moment to thank God for the gifts of science and religion and for the talents you have for exploring both.

CHAPTER 10

A World
in Turmoil
A.D. 1789–1814

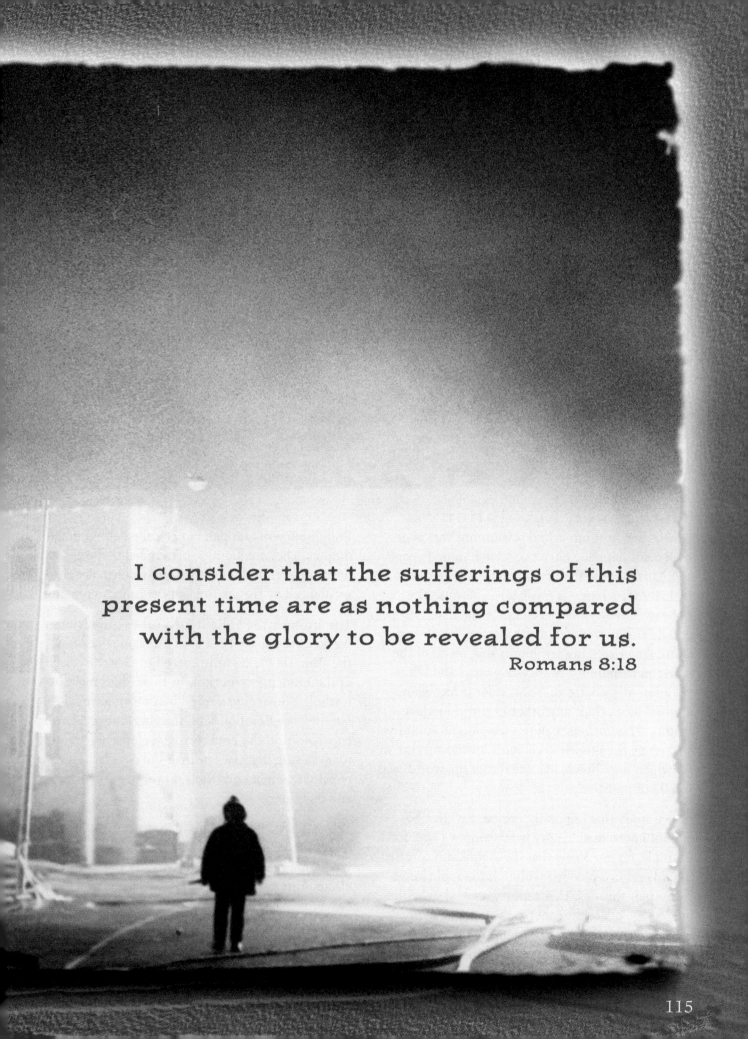

I consider that the sufferings of this present time are as nothing compared with the glory to be revealed for us.

Romans 8:18

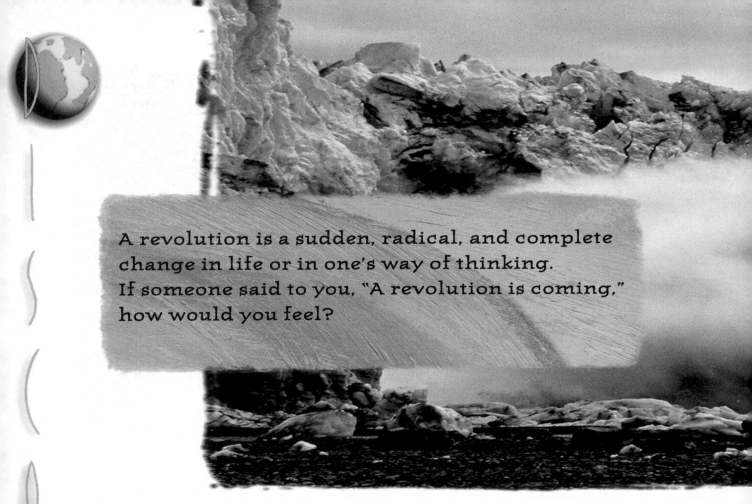

A revolution is a sudden, radical, and complete change in life or in one's way of thinking. If someone said to you, "A revolution is coming," how would you feel?

The French Revolution

One of the most important revolutions that ever took place happened just over two hundred years ago. This was the French Revolution, which began in 1789. The name is misleading because the upheaval involved not just France but all of Europe, and its effects were felt as far away as North and South America. This revolution kept much of the world in turmoil for twenty-five years and left it permanently changed. No wonder it has been studied more than any other event in modern history. The Catholic Church was also profoundly shaken by the French Revolution. It was a revolution for which the Church, like the rest of the world, was totally unprepared.

As we study this important period, we must be careful not to read history backward. In 1750, for example, no one knew that the eighteenth century would end in a bloody revolution to topple kings from their thrones. That century seemed to be the golden age of absolute monarchs (rulers who had complete authority). As the century progressed, many of these monarchs absorbed the ideas of the

Enlightenment and liked to be called enlightened despots. They frequently surrounded themselves with advisors and officials who had been deeply influenced by the writings of the Enlightenment.

The stronger the enlightened rulers grew, the weaker the papacy became. This is one reason why the Church was so unprepared to face the crisis of the French Revolution. In those days most of Catholic Europe was ruled by two rival royal families, the Bourbons and the Hapsburgs. At every papal election the Bourbons and Hapsburgs plotted to make sure that the cardinals did not elect a strong pope who might curb their power over the Church and its leaders.

The result was that the eighteenth-century popes tended to be elderly and feeble caretakers who would not make any waves. In 1721 the cardinals elected Innocent XIII (1721–1724), a man who two years earlier had resigned as bishop of a small Italian diocese because he was too ill to administer it. Another pope, Clement XII (1730–1740),

seventy-nine years old at his election, was blind and often bedridden for the last eight years of his pontificate.

The clearest example of the weakness of the popes in this period is their treatment of the Jesuits. The Jesuits had many enemies. Those who supported the Enlightenment disliked them because they were its most effective Catholic critics. In South America greedy landowners hated them because they protected the Indians from enslavement. Some narrow-minded Catholics called Jansenists were horrified that the Jesuits preferred to emphasize God's love and mercy rather than fear of death and hell.

The most powerful opponents of the Jesuits, however, were the Catholic monarchs of Europe. They objected to the Jesuits' loyalty to the pope. Consequently, beginning in 1759, the Jesuits were expelled from Portugal, then from France, Spain, and much of Italy. Finally, in 1773, Pope Clement XIV (1769–1774) suppressed the Society of Jesus throughout the world. He explained that he did it "for the peace of the Church," meaning that he wanted to please the Catholic monarchs of Europe. With friends like Clement XIV, the Jesuits hardly needed enemies.

The suppression of the Jesuits was a terrible blow to the Catholic Church everywhere. The Society of Jesus was forced to abandon hundreds of Catholic colleges precisely at the time that the Church needed educated leaders to combat the antireligious influences of the Enlightenment. Thousands of Jesuit missionaries were expelled from the Portuguese, Spanish, and French empires. This severely crippled the missionary work of the Church. Most of all, it indicated that Catholics would not be able to count on much leadership from the top when the storm of the French Revolution broke over the Church.

 Why is strong leadership so important for the Church?

117

March of the female army to Versailles, engraving, 1789

Revolution and the Church

Besides weak leadership, what other seeds of revolution were ready to sprout in France? Let's look back and see.

On May 4, 1789, a magnificent spectacle took place at Versailles, the splendid palace that King Louis XIV had built a few miles from Paris, the French capital. On that spring day a colorful procession of bishops, priests, nobles, lawyers, and businessmen wound their way through the palace grounds to the royal chapel for the celebration of Mass. The occasion was the opening session of the Estates-General (the French legislature). The clergy occupied the most prominent and prestigious places in the procession that day. They were the First Estate and outranked the Second Estate (the nobility) and the Third Estate (the commoners).

King Louis XVI (who reigned from 1774 to 1793) had assembled the Estates-General merely to obtain more taxes. However, he soon lost control of events to the leaders of the Third Estate, who had their own ideas about what changes were needed in France. No one knew it at the time, but that day was the beginning of the French Revolution.

The Catholic Church occupied such an important place in French life that it could hardly escape being touched by these winds of change. One historian compared the Church in France at that time to a great old oak tree that looked strong and sturdy on the outside but had actually been weakened from within by rot and disease. It would require only one strong gust of wind to bring the whole structure crashing to the ground.

The battle cry of the revolutionists was "liberty, equality, fraternity," a motto that still appears on all French coins. There is nothing anti-Christian about that motto, and at first many Catholics strongly supported the Revolution. In fact parish priests played a crucial role at its start. In May and June of 1789, there was a standoff at Versailles between the Second and Third Estates. The priests in the First Estate held the balance of power. They threw in their lot with the Third Estate and transformed the Estates-General into a one-house National Assembly.

Many Americans think of the French Revolution as one long bloodbath, but that is a distorted view.

CATHOLIC ID

In the 1790s few Catholic bishops favored democracy. One of the few who did was Barnaba Chiaramonti, the bishop of Imola in Italy. Eventually he was elected pope and took the name of Pius VII.

There was little violence during the first two years, when the National Assembly governed France. The members of that body were mostly lawyers and businessmen who hated bloodshed. They wanted to give France the same kind of government that England had, a constitutional monarchy in which the king's power would be limited by an elected parliament.

The National Assembly did not want to destroy the Catholic Church. Rather, it wanted to control the Church even more completely than the absolute monarchs had done. The assembly abolished the taxes the Church collected and took possession of all church property. These changes made the Church dependent on the government. Few Catholics raised any protest or objected when the National Assembly abolished the monastic orders.

A New Decree

In July 1790 the National Assembly issued a decree that drove a fatal wedge between the revolutionists and the Catholic Church. This decree was the Civil Constitution of the Clergy, which was designed to regulate Church affairs in the new constitutional monarchy. There was to be a drastic rearrangement of dioceses and parishes; pastors and bishops were to be elected by the "people" (really by the wealthier taxpayers). Neither the king nor the pope was to have any role in the selection of bishops.

In November 1790 the assembly required bishops and priests to take an oath accepting this decree. Each of them had to decide whether or not to take this oath. Many of them looked to the pope for guidance, but Pope Pius VI (1775–1799) said nothing. Only a few bishops accepted the Civil Constitution, but about half of the French priests did so. They formed the new constitutional Church, and the other bishops and priests were driven from their posts. The Catholic Church in France was now in schism. There were two Churches in France, each claiming to be the real Catholic Church. One was allied with the government; the other was in opposition to it.

Finally, in the spring of 1791, the pope spoke. When he did so, Pius VI condemned not just the Civil Constitution of the Clergy but the whole course of the Revolution up to that point. He denounced the National Assembly for ignoring God and introducing an unlimited freedom that allowed people to think, say, and publish anything they wished about religion, whether it was true or not. The French Revolution and the Catholic Church were on a collision course. The Revolution itself soon became more radical and bloody, and one of its victims was to be the Catholic Church.

Does any government have the right to control the Church? Why or why not?

The Reign of Terror

Between 1793 and 1794 the French Revolution entered upon its most violent phase. During this bloody period a republic was proclaimed, the king was executed, revolts broke out in many parts of the country, and all of Europe went to war with France. Few thought that the French Republic could survive. But survive it did, thanks to the efforts of the famous Committee of Public Safety, which organized new armies that won the war. To crush all opposition within France, the Committee of Public Safety also organized a bloody campaign of repression that has gone down in history as the *Reign of Terror.*

Perhaps as many as forty thousand people died during the Terror. Victims included royalists, nobles, political moderates, priests, nuns—anyone whose loyalty to the Republic was suspect. Antireligious fanatics used the opportunity to launch an all-out attack on the Catholic Church. The National Assembly had tried to control the Church; these fanatics wanted to destroy it. Their object was literally to dechristianize France. The Church had not seen anything like this since the persecutions under the pagan Roman emperors.

Any priest could be arrested and was likely to be executed if he was denounced by six people for being a bad citizen. Thousands of priests fled the country to save their lives. Some were not so lucky; between two thousand and five thousand priests were killed. There was also widespread vandalism of Church property. Church buildings were turned into barracks and stables; vestments were ripped up and used as bandages; donkeys were given drink from chalices. These and other unthinkable things were done against the Church.

Priests were pressured into renouncing their priesthood. New religions were encouraged by the government as a substitute for Christianity. Perhaps the most anti-Christian measure of all was a new calendar designed to wipe out the memory of Sundays and holy days. Finally the Reign of Terror came to an end, in July 1794, when even officials of the government began to fear that they might be its next victims.

Church and State

From 1795 to 1799 France was governed by the Directory, which avoided bloodshed but was very unfriendly to the Church. There was strict separation of Church and state, but that did not mean what it means in the United States today, where separation is a friendly arrangement that has assured religious freedom for all. The Directory gave Catholics religious toleration, but someone said that it was tossed to them like a coin to a beggar. Moreover, church buildings were owned by the government, and Catholics had to take a loyalty oath in order to use them. Police spies often attended Mass to be sure that the priest did not say anything critical of the government.

The Church of Ste. Geneviève was renamed the Pantheon and turned into a memorial to great Frenchmen.

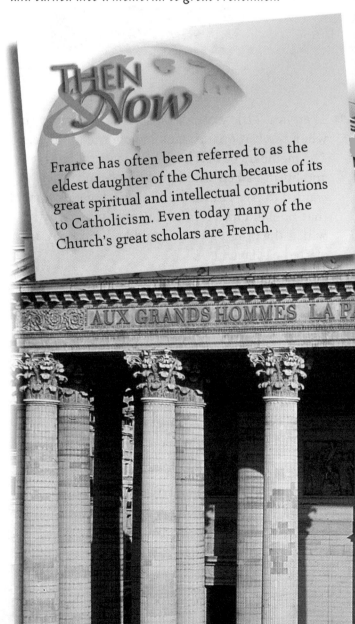

France has often been referred to as the eldest daughter of the Church because of its great spiritual and intellectual contributions to Catholicism. Even today many of the Church's great scholars are French.

How did the French revolutionaries attack the Church?

During the Directory French armies conquered the Dutch Netherlands, Switzerland, and much of Italy. In all these places the old rulers fled, and the French introduced new revolutionary governments. Conditions varied from one place to the next, depending on the French general who was in charge of the area. Some of these generals were very antireligious; others made an effort to be friendly to the Church. One of the friendly generals was a man in his twenties named Napoleone Buonaparte (1769–1821). He was quickly becoming the most successful general in the French army and one of the most admired men in France.

One of the places conquered and occupied by the French army was Rome. In 1798 the French proclaimed a Roman Republic and banished Pope Pius VI from the city. The following year they arrested the eighty-two-year-old pontiff and deported him to France. He died a prisoner in 1799. Many thought that he would be the last pope and that the Catholic Church would not long survive him.

There was no pope for the next seven months, and the state of the Catholic Church was worse than it had been for many centuries. The French Revolution by this time had reached many of the most Catholic areas of Europe and caused widespread disruption of religious life. Rome itself was occupied by several different warring armies. Under such conditions it was impossible to hold a papal election there.

Meanwhile, in France, the Directory was more unpopular than ever. Some of the leading officials of the government decided that it was time for still another change. They planned to use the popular young General Buonaparte for their own purposes. They overthrew the Directory and gave Buonaparte a fancy title, but they intended to treat him like a puppet. Instead, these politicians got the surprise of their lives.

 How was it possible for French Catholics to remain faithful during the Reign of Terror?

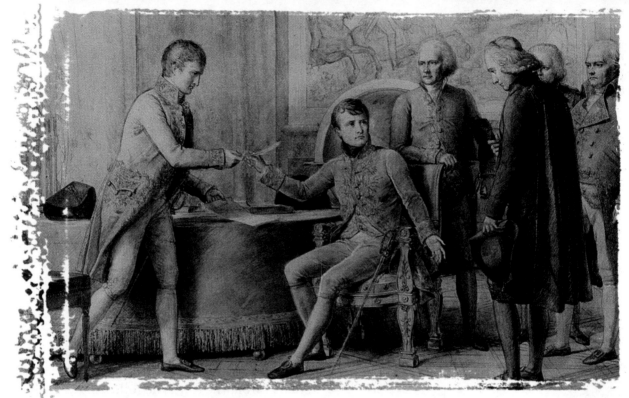

Napoleon signs the Concordat of 1801 with Pope Pius VII, Gérard, 19th century

A New Pope

Between 1800 and 1814 two men controlled the fate of the Catholic Church. One was Napoleon Bonaparte (as he now spelled his name); the other was Pope Pius VII (1800–1823). Napoleon came to power first, in November 1799. He brushed aside the politicians who had supported him and made himself the undisputed ruler of France. He promised the French people peace, and he delivered on his promise. Part of his program was religious peace; and to accomplish this, Napoleon knew that he needed the cooperation of the pope. However, there was no pope at this time.

The papacy was vacant from the death of Pius VI on August 29, 1799, until March 14, 1800, when a former monk named Barnaba Chiaramonti was elected and took the name of Pius VII. In the whole history of the Catholic Church, few popes have assumed their office under more depressing circumstances. Even the papal election had to be held in the city of Venice because Rome was too unsafe. Pius VII proved to be one of the greatest of all modern popes. This is especially true when we remember that he began with a Church that was in ruins practically everywhere.

Napoleon was not a religious person, but he wanted peace with the Church because it would make him popular with French Catholics. He said to a French diplomat, "Tell the Holy Father that I wish to make him a present of twenty-five million Frenchmen." Pius VII responded positively, and negotiations began for a treaty between the pope and Napoleon.

Concordat and Conflict

The result was the *Concordat* (treaty) *of 1801*. Both sides got important benefits from the concordat. Napoleon won the support of French Catholics, and the Catholics of France obtained religious freedom. The real winner was the pope. Why? Because Napoleon recognized him as the leader of the Church. At Napoleon's request Pius VII appointed new French bishops.

The concordat was a huge success, and the Catholic Church began a remarkable recovery. All over France and French-occupied Europe, church buildings were reopened, and millions of Catholics flocked to religious services. Every year thereafter the government added to its financial support of the Church. Vocations to the priesthood started to increase, and slowly but surely the religious orders reappeared.

The high point of the cooperation between Napoleon and Pius VII occurred in 1804, when the pope went to Paris for the coronation of Napoleon as emperor of the French.

Napoleon, however, was not completely trustworthy, and the honeymoon with Pius VII did not last. Blinded by a desire for power, Napoleon soon embarked on a series of wars and expanded the French Empire until it included much of Europe. The one country that Napoleon could not defeat was England, which was protected by the sea and by its "wooden walls," the ships of the Royal Navy. A furious Napoleon ordered all the countries of Europe to join him in an alliance against England. The pope refused on the grounds that he had no quarrel with the English.

Napoleon retaliated in 1809 by seizing the pope and carrying him off to France, where he remained a prisoner until 1814. Pius VII fought back with the only means available to him: He refused to function as pope and lived as a simple monk. His resistance to Napoleon earned him enormous respect throughout

Europe. Few other people had the courage to stand up to Napoleon as Pope Pius VII did.

In 1814 Napoleon was finally defeated and exiled to the little island of Elba. Pius VII returned to Rome in triumph. It was an astonishing turnaround for the papacy. The earlier popes had been weak; Pius VI had died in 1799, abandoned in a French prison. Now, fifteen years later, his successor was hailed as a hero throughout the world by Catholics and non-Catholics alike.

One of Pius VII's closest friends, Cardinal Consalvi, advised the pope that the world had been profoundly changed by the French Revolution and that it would be impossible to turn the calendar back to the year 1789. He told the pope that people, especially young people, would no longer think the same way.

This was wise advice. For the next hundred years, Church history would be largely the story of the Church trying to come to grips with the new world created by the French Revolution.

A beautiful prayer to say during times of conflict and recovery is Psalm 23. Make it part of your prayer this week.

Napoleon crowns himself emperor, David, 1805–1807

things to think about

Why do you think the French Revolution is such an important time in Church history?

How would you compare the dechristianization campaign of the French Revolution with the persecution that the Church experienced during the Roman Empire?

things to share

Explain to someone why Napoleon was both a friend and an enemy of the Church.

How would you help someone to see where God was at work in the Church after the terrible years of the French Revolution?

WORDS TO REMEMBER

Find and define the following:

Reign of Terror _____
_____
_____

Concordat of 1801 _____
_____
_____

OnLine
WITH THE PARISH

We American Catholics have been blessed with a government that has treated us fairly. However, can you think of any moral or social issues that it would be appropriate for priests to mention in church and that would challenge our government?

What does the suppression of the Jesuits in the eighteenth century tell us about the state of the Catholic Church before the French Revolution?

1

What conditions helped to bring about the French Revolution?

2

How did the National Assembly in France try to control the Church?

3

How was the Church affected by the Reign of Terror?

4

Life
in the Spirit

In 1789 the motto "liberty, equality, fraternity" sounded very radical and scared many Catholics, including Pope Pius VI. He responded by condemning the whole French Revolution. However, on his visit to France in 1980, Pope John Paul II praised that famous motto of the French Revolution. He said, "We know the place held in your culture and your history by the ideas of liberty, equality, and fraternity. In fact, these are Christian ideas." Ask the Holy Spirit to help you put these ideas into practice in your life.

Why was Napoleon eager to make peace with the Church?

5

CHAPTER 11

THE DAWN
OF A NEW AGE
A.D. 1814–1914

The Church shows forth the kingship
of Christ over all creation.
Pope Leo XIII

Some people welcome change; others resist it. Which type of person are you? Do you accept change well?

A World at Peace

In the spring of 1814, great celebrations were held all over Europe. The French Revolution was over. Now there was much talk of the "good old days" before the Revolution, when kings and emperors had preserved law and order and kept Europe at peace. Many people dreamed of bringing back those days. However, the world is never the same twice, and it is never really possible to bring back the past. As we noted before, the most important revolution that had taken place was in people's minds. And there was no way to undo that change.

The French Revolution gave a great boost to two powerful movements of thought that were to gather strength throughout the nineteenth century. One was called liberalism, and the other was called nationalism. Both are difficult to define.

Even today they mean different things to different people. Two hundred years ago in Europe, these words had a different meaning than they do in America today.

Liberalism   *Liberalism* was the creed of those who wanted more freedom, the kind of freedoms that we enjoy under our Bill of Rights. These include freedom of speech, of the press, and of religion and the right to assemble peacefully. Today most Americans would wonder why anyone would ever have been afraid of giving people greater freedom. Two hundred years ago, however, it was a different story. Many people, including many Catholics, feared that such freedom would be abused and would lead once again to violence and bloodshed.

Catholics had reasons to be suspicious of liberalism. Many liberals of that time were quite antireligious. They had been educated in the anti-Christian writings of the Enlightenment. Rightly or wrongly Catholics regarded liberals as people for whom freedom meant the right to do anything they pleased, regardless of God's commandments.

Nationalism *Nationalism* is equally difficult to define. In its highest and best sense, it is patriotism, the virtue of loving one's country. No Catholic could be opposed to that kind of nationalism. However, nationalism can also be cruel and ugly when it turns into hatred and intolerance of other countries and other nationalities. No sincere Christian can embrace that kind of nationalism.

During the nineteenth century there were many bitter battles between Catholics and liberals or nationalists. The conflict was especially severe in Italy, where nationalists seized the Papal States and established a liberal Italian kingdom. Pope Pius IX refused to recognize the new Italy and in 1870 closed himself off in the Vatican.

Germany was unified in 1871 by Otto von Bismarck (1815–1898), who then proceeded to launch a persecution of the Catholic Church in the new German Empire. In France after 1879 the government became increasingly hostile to the Church, leading in 1905 to the separation of Church and state on terms very unfavorable to the Church. Similar disputes occurred in other countries.

Not all Catholics thought that this kind of conflict was certain to happen. In France a talented young priest named Félicité de Lamennais (1782–1854) urged Catholics to take a more favorable look at what was good in liberalism and nationalism. He was condemned for doing so by Pope Gregory XVI (1831–1846), left the Church, and died a bitter man. However, he left behind a whole host of admirers who brought new life to the Catholic Church in France. In Belgium, Poland, England, Ireland, and elsewhere, Catholics often found that they had much in common with liberals or nationalists and worked together to improve people's lives.

 What does freedom of religion mean to you?

Sister of Mercy today

An Age of Faith

Even though the Church had to deal with unfriendly governments, the nineteenth century was a great age of faith. The Catholic Church enjoyed a spectacular spiritual revival. Why was this so?

First of all there were more Catholics than ever before in history. By 1914 almost one out of every three people in the world was a European, and many of them were Catholics. The number of Catholics also increased dramatically in both North and South America. The nineteenth century was also one of the great missionary eras in Church history. This activity led to the spread of Catholicism throughout much of Asia and Africa.

When we look at the religious orders during this period, we see that it was a time of amazing growth. The old religious orders such as the Franciscans, Dominicans, Benedictines, and Jesuits recovered from the brutality of the French Revolution. Even more amazing was the number of new religious orders—such as the Marists, Salesians, and Oblates of Mary Immaculate—that were founded. They sprang up everywhere.

Most amazing of all was the growth in the number of women religious. Never before or since in the

history of the Church have there been so many nuns and sisters. By the close of the nineteenth century, there were about one million members of religious orders, the great majority of them women. Many women joined religious communities such as the Ursulines, Sisters of Saint Joseph, Sisters of Mercy, and Sisters of Charity.

Still other men and women joined a new kind of order dedicated exclusively to the foreign missions. Every country had at least one missionary order, such as the Society of the African Missions in France, the Mill Hill Fathers in England, the Columban Fathers in Ireland, and the Maryknoll Fathers, Brothers, and Sisters in the United States.

All this growth made possible a vast expansion of Catholic educational and charitable activity. For the first time in history, an effort was made to provide education for all children. Catholic priests, brothers, and sisters participated in this effort by opening academies for the rich and free schools for the poor. They also established a huge network of Catholic hospitals, orphanages, old-age homes, and other charitable institutions.

The Laity

The Catholic laity, who were now better educated and better organized than ever before, also showed amazing signs of spiritual life. Their activities varied from country to country. Let's take a look at a few examples. In Germany lay Catholics organized their own political party, the Center Party, which led the defense of Catholic rights against Bismarck. In France a devout layman named Frédéric Ozanam (1813–1853) founded the Saint Vincent de Paul Society, whose members visited the poor in their homes and took a personal interest in helping them.

In Ireland another layman, Daniel O'Connell (1775–1847), founded the Catholic Association to obtain civil rights for Irish and English Catholics. O'Connell pioneered the peaceful civil rights techniques that later would be used by Mohandas Gandhi in India and by Dr. Martin Luther King, Jr., in the United States. O'Connell was also a good example of a Catholic who could be both a liberal and a nationalist without being untrue to his religion. He wanted civil rights for all people, not just his fellow Irish Catholics.

During this time devotion to the Sacred Heart of Jesus was also very popular. It was promoted especially by the Jesuits. They wisely related this devotion to the Eucharist by encouraging Catholics to receive Holy Communion on the first Friday of every month. As the century was coming to a close, Pope Leo XIII dedicated the whole world to the Sacred Heart in 1899.

Devotion to the Blessed Virgin Mary was extremely popular, fostered by such developments as the 1854 proclamation by Pope Pius IX of the doctrine of the Immaculate Conception of Mary. Pope Leo XIII encouraged the recitation of the rosary, and special Marian devotions were held in May and October in many parish churches. Pilgrimages, which had practically disappeared in the eighteenth century, now became more popular than ever. Thousands traveled every year to Rome and to Marian shrines such as Lourdes.

In every age the real history of the Church takes place in the hearts and souls of countless ordinary Catholics. There were so many external signs of life in the Church that there can be little doubt that in the nineteenth century the Catholic Church was alive and well on this deeper level also.

 Try to get more information about the Maryknoll missioners and other mission communities.

Immaculate Conception, *Murillo, 17th century*

CATHOLIC **ID**
Pope Pius X once asked some of the cardinals what they thought the Church needed most. One said, "More schools." Another said, "More churches." A third said, "More priests." The pope replied, "No, what we need most are well-informed and virtuous laypeople in each parish."

Missionary Activity

The nineteenth century was a great age of missionary activity among both Protestants and Catholics. There are several obvious reasons why this was so. Improvements in communication and transportation made it easier for missionaries to travel to the farthest corners of the globe. Modern medicine helped them to survive the hazards of tropical diseases. And there was no lack of volunteers to spread the gospel. The religious revival in Europe produced thousands of enthusiastic young men and women who were eager to leave home and to risk their lives abroad for the sake of the kingdom.

Among Catholics the new missionary orders attracted many recruits, and the Congregation for the Propagation of the Faith raised large sums to finance their work. Pope Gregory XVI had served as head of the Propagation of the Faith before becoming pope. As pope he continued to take a deep interest in the missions and to encourage their expansion.

Among Catholic nations France provided most of the missionaries. By 1900 two-thirds of Catholic missionaries were French. They were active not only in the French empire but all over the world, including the United States, which was officially considered a missionary country by Rome until 1908.

French missionaries made an invaluable contribution to the evangelization of the American West in the late nineteenth century. At the other end of the United States, in a cemetery in St. Augustine, Florida, one can still see the gravestones of the young Sisters of Saint Joseph who came from France to minister to the freed slaves after the Civil War and who died from yellow fever.

One of the most touching stories involves some French missionaries who arrived in Japan in 1865. Japan had been cut off from contact with the outside world for two centuries. However, these French missionaries discovered isolated little communities of Japanese Catholics who had kept the faith alive since the seventeenth century without priests or the Eucharist. At first these Japanese Catholics were suspicious of the French missionaries. They finally accepted the French priests as real Catholics when they were sure that the priests were unmarried, that they accepted the authority of the pope, and that they venerated the Blessed Virgin Mary.

A Mixed Blessing

The second half of the nineteenth century was a new age of imperialism, when the great powers of Europe again took an interest in acquiring colonies all over the world. Beginning in the 1880s, the European nations carved up the whole continent of Africa for themselves. It was the age when the English could boast that the sun never set on the British Empire. This new imperialism was a mixed blessing for the Christian missions.

European governments provided protection for the Christian missionaries, but it was sometimes hard to separate the cross from the flag. Even the best-intentioned missionaries sometimes found it difficult to remember that their primary purpose was to spread the gospel, not to promote the interests of their mother country.

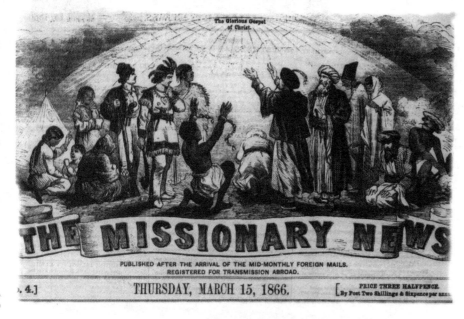

The Glorious Gospel of Christ.

THE MISSIONARY NEWS

PUBLISHED AFTER THE ARRIVAL OF THE MID-MONTHLY FOREIGN MAILS.
REGISTERED FOR TRANSMISSION ABROAD.

., 4.]   THURSDAY, MARCH 15, 1866.   [PRICE THREE HALFPENCE.
[By Post Two Shillings & Sixpence per ann.

Franciscan missionaries working with young people

Another complaint about some nineteenth-century missionaries was that they looked down on the native peoples of Asia and Africa as inferior to the Europeans. Even in China, with a civilization much older than that of Europe, some missionaries claimed that the Chinese lacked the intelligence to become priests.

In 1919 Pope Benedict XV (1914–1922) issued a document in which he told the missionaries to remember that their job was to spread the Christian faith, not to promote European colonialism. The pope also told them to respect the cultures of non-European peoples and to encourage native vocations to the priesthood.

The next two popes built on the work of Benedict XV. In 1926 Pope Pius XI (1922–1939) consecrated six Chinese bishops at a spectacular ceremony in Rome. In 1939 Pope Pius XII (1939–1958) consecrated a dozen bishops from all over the world, including two black bishops from Africa. At the time of the closing of the Second Vatican Council in 1965, there were no fewer than 160 Asian bishops and 68 African bishops. The Catholic Church seemed more truly "catholic" than it had been for a long time.

 If you could do missionary work anywhere in the world, where would it be, and what would you do?

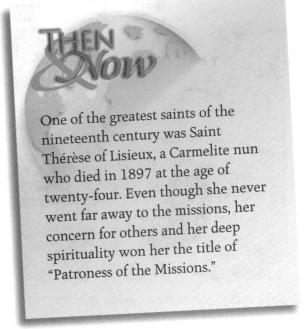

THEN & NOW

One of the greatest saints of the nineteenth century was Saint Thérèse of Lisieux, a Carmelite nun who died in 1897 at the age of twenty-four. Even though she never went far away to the missions, her concern for others and her deep spirituality won her the title of "Patroness of the Missions."

New Role of the Papacy

One of the most important popes in history was Pius IX, who led the Church for thirty-two years (1846–1878), longer than any other pontiff in the long history of the Catholic Church. He was an embattled pope, constantly at odds with anti-Catholic liberals and nationalists. The more difficulties Pius IX suffered, the more sympathy he received from Catholics throughout the world, especially after the loss of the Papal States to the new Italian kingdom.

During his pontificate there was a major change in the way that the Catholic Church was governed. More and more Catholics looked directly to him for leadership and guidance, rather than to their own bishops. This process reached a peak at the First Vatican Council (1869–1870), when the assembled bishops defined the doctrine that the most solemn statements of the pope on matters of faith and morals are infallible. This meant that such statements enjoy a divine guarantee that they are free from error.

Pope Pius X, known for his encouragement of frequent reception of Holy Communion

Pius IX's successor was another long-lived pontiff, Leo XIII (1878–1903). He was sixty-eight years old at the time of his election as pope and died at the age of ninety-three, having outlived all but one of the cardinals who had elected him. The first pope born after the French Revolution, Leo was more in tune with the modern world than his predecessor had been. He adopted a different style of leadership and soon solved problems that had dragged on for years under Pius IX.

Leo was the first pope to recognize the social problems caused by the Industrial Revolution. All over Europe millions of workers were living in hopeless poverty, taken advantage of by greedy businessmen, while their governments did nothing to help. It is no wonder that many workers turned to socialism and communism as their only hope for a better life.

This was the background to the most famous of Leo's eighty-five encyclicals, *Rerum Novarum* ("Of New Things"), which appeared in 1891. In that document the pope took the side of the oppressed workers, defending their right to form labor unions and calling on governments to protect them. Today the language of the encyclical seems mild, but in 1891 it was something of a bombshell and shocked many wealthy businessmen.

Pope Pius X and the Liturgy

When Leo XIII died in 1903, the cardinals elected as his successor Joseph Sarto, a man of humble origins who had spent most of his life as a parish priest and diocesan bishop. He took the name of Pius X. Although he only lived until 1914, Pius X made his mark on the Church in many ways. He was very popular in his lifetime, and he is the only pope of the past two centuries to be canonized.

Perhaps his outstanding contribution to the Church was the two changes that he made with regard to the Eucharist. First, he urged people to receive Holy Communion frequently, even daily. Until then even the most pious laypeople rarely received Holy Communion more than a few times a year out of a mistaken sense of reverence for the Eucharist. Second, he said that children should no

longer be kept from receiving Holy Communion. They should be able to make their First Holy Communion as soon as they understood the difference between bread and the Eucharist.

Pius X did something else that would eventually lead to a revolution in the way that Catholics worship. He objected to the elaborate music that was often played at Mass. He said that the music should help people to pray and therefore should be simple music so that all the people could sing.

The pope's comments went well beyond the question of music. He stated that parishioners should be able to participate actively in the celebration of Mass. In order for them to do so, some thought that the Mass would have to be celebrated in their own language, not in Latin. Pius X would certainly not have approved of such a change of language, but he sowed the seeds that eventually and logically led to that change at the Second Vatican Council. That change was also radical in the sense that it was a return to the ancient tradition of celebrating the Mass in the language of the people.

"God writes straight with crooked lines" is an old proverb that means God sometimes uses strange means to accomplish his purposes. Pope Saint

Pius X is a good example. He was very conservative and old-fashioned in many ways, but he set in motion some far-reaching changes in the Church.

 Choose which nineteenth-century pope you would like to have met and tell why.

PERSONAL PROFILE

John Henry Newman (1801–1890) was probably the most prominent Catholic in the English-speaking world in the nineteenth century. Born in England, he spent the first half of his life as a member and then a clergyman of the Church of England, a Church for which he always kept a deep regard. Newman became a Catholic in 1845 and spent most of the rest of his life as a priest in the city of Birmingham, England. He reached a worldwide audience through his books, sermons, essays, and letters. These writings are still read with great interest today. In 1879 Pope Leo XIII made Newman a cardinal.

PUTTING IT TOGETHER

things
to think about

Many consider the nineteenth century a great age of faith. Do you agree? If so, what reasons can you give for saying that it was an age when the Catholic Church experienced a remarkable spiritual revival?

What do historians mean when they say that the Catholic Church was more "catholic" in 1900 than it was in 1800?

things
to share

Someone says to you that the Church should go back and be the way it was in the 1950s. Your response?

Share your thoughts on the following statement: The real history of the Church takes place in the hearts and souls of ordinary Catholics.

WORDS TO REMEMBER

Find and define the following:

liberalism _____
_____
_____

nationalism _____
_____
_____

OnLine
WITH THE PARISH

What efforts does your parish make to help people participate actively in the celebration of the Eucharist? Have you ever thought of volunteering as an altar server, lector, or Eucharist minister? Why not do so?

Give two reasons why the nineteenth century was a great age for the missions.

1

Who was Daniel O'Connell, and why is he sometimes compared with Dr. Martin Luther King, Jr.?

2

Why was Pope Pius IX one of the most important popes of the nineteenth century?

3

When can nationalism become a false ideal?

4

Why is Leo XIII one of the great popes of modern times?

5

Life in the Spirit

Saint Thérèse of Lisieux (1873–1897) became famous after her death because she left behind a little book, *The History of a Soul*, in which she described her way to holiness. She called it her "little way," and she explained that it consisted of doing the everyday things of life as perfectly as she could out of love for God and neighbor. One day you may wish to read this book. Meanwhile ask Saint Thérèse to pray that you may do everyday things as perfectly as possible.

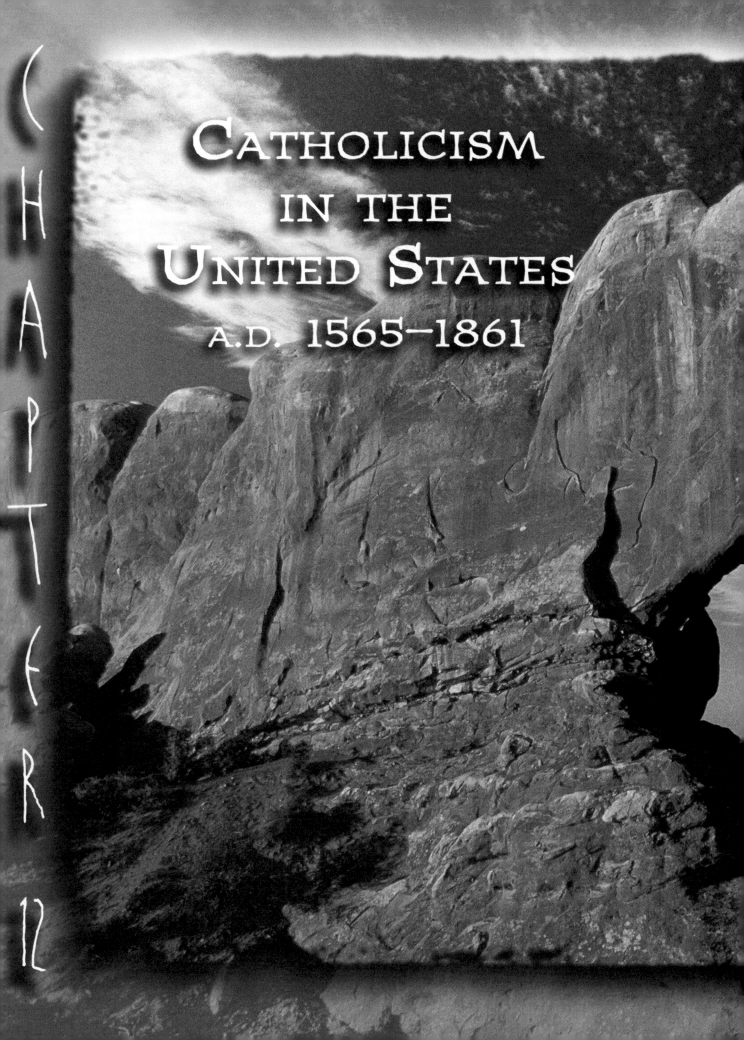

CATHOLICISM
IN THE
UNITED STATES
A.D. 1565–1861

CHAPTER 12

May this People
be long in life
and increase.
Ancient Arapaho Invocation

Does Catholicism have a history in the United States? Where do we begin to tell the story of the Catholic Church in our own country?

San Carlos Mission, Monterey-Carmel, established in 1770 by Junípero Serra

The Spanish Impact

The United States of America is now more than 220 years old, but American history goes back even further than that. During the two centuries before 1776, the history of North America was largely the story of three European countries—Spain, France, and England—struggling with one another and with the Native Americans for the control of the New World. Each of these European countries also contributed to the beginnings of Catholicism in what later became the United States. Because the Spanish came here first, let's begin with them.

California, Texas, and Florida, three of the largest states, were once part of a huge Spanish arc. That arc stretched across North America from the Pacific Northwest to the Gulf Coast. In 1565 the Spanish established their first North American colony in St. Augustine, Florida. St. Augustine is the oldest city in the United States, and it also contains the oldest Catholic parish, Nombre de Dios ("Name of God"). Although the Spanish remained in Florida for over

two hundred years, few of them settled there permanently.

Texas was even bigger than Florida, and there, too, the Spanish had little permanent impact. They established a few military posts and missions for the Indians, including the famous mission in San Antonio, founded in 1718. However, the Spanish faced challenging problems in Texas. The distances were vast, the Native Americans spoke a bewildering variety of languages, and few Europeans wished to live there.

Incredible as it may seem to us today, even California received little attention from the Spanish. In fact they regarded it as the Siberia of their empire. As late as 1846 there were only four thousand Europeans there. The Spanish only began to settle the area in 1769, when they feared that the Russians, advancing south from Alaska, might beat them to the punch. Junípero Serra (1713–1784), a Franciscan friar, was appointed to establish a string

140

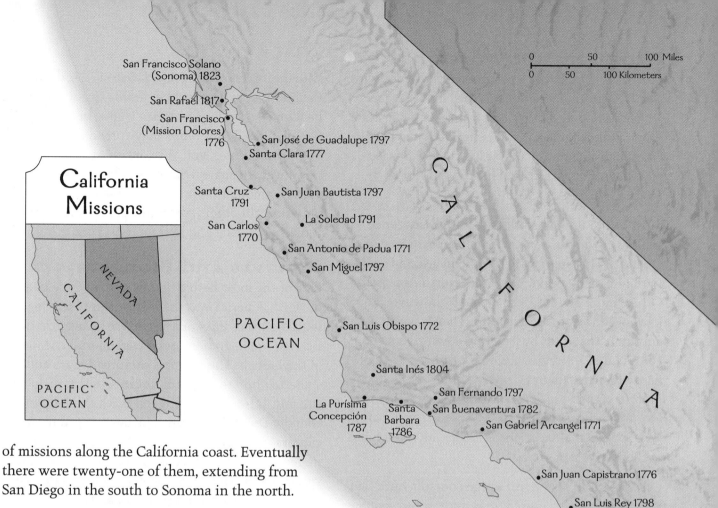

California Missions

San Francisco Solano (Sonoma) 1823
San Rafael 1817
San Francisco (Mission Dolores) 1776
San José de Guadalupe 1797
Santa Clara 1777
Santa Cruz 1791
San Juan Bautista 1797
San Carlos 1770
La Soledad 1791
San Antonio de Padua 1771
San Miguel 1797
San Luis Obispo 1772
Santa Inés 1804
La Purísima Concepción 1787
Santa Barbara 1786
San Fernando 1797
San Buenaventura 1782
San Gabriel Arcangel 1771
San Juan Capistrano 1776
San Luis Rey 1798
San Diego 1769

PACIFIC OCEAN

CALIFORNIA

NEVADA

PACIFIC OCEAN

0   50   100 Miles
0   50   100 Kilometers

of missions along the California coast. Eventually there were twenty-one of them, extending from San Diego in the south to Sonoma in the north.

The California missions contained not only churches but also homes, schools, workshops, warehouses, farms, and ranches for the Indians. For many years the friars were widely admired for what they did on behalf of the Indians in these missions. Today, however, they are often criticized because they treated the Indians like children and gave them little opportunity for growth in self-reliance. Both praise and criticism are justified, but it is only fair to judge the California missions by the standards of that time, not our own.

Another person who deserves to rank with Serra as an outstanding missionary was the Jesuit Eusebio Kino (1645–1711). As a young priest, he wanted to go to China. Instead he was sent to Mexico, where he made his way to the northern part of the country. There he established the mission of Nuestra Señora de los Dolores ("Our Lady of Sorrows"). With that mission as his headquarters from 1687 to 1711, Kino traveled constantly on horseback throughout the surrounding region, journeying as far as the area that is present-day Arizona. He was a missionary, pastor, explorer, mapmaker, historian, and protector of the Indians.

The Spanish had their greatest impact in the area that is now New Mexico. They founded the city of Santa Fe in 1610 and made many converts among the Pueblo Indians. When New Mexico became part of the United States in 1848, the territory contained some fifty thousand Catholics, Spanish, Native Americans, and people of mixed blood. To this day New Mexico proudly retains much of its Spanish culture and heritage.

As the United States expanded its boundaries to the Pacific in the early nineteenth century, it took in these vast areas that had once been part of the Spanish arc. New American missionaries (often French-born) arrived with the settlers from the eastern United States. In almost every place, however, these American missionaries were not starting fresh. They were building on foundations that had been laid centuries before by Spanish missionaries.

141

Explorers and Missionaries

Like Spain, France once possessed a vast empire in North America. Its center was the city of Quebec, which was founded in 1608 by Samuel de Champlain. A few years later the first missionaries arrived. One small community of priests, called Sulpicians, played a major role in establishing the city of Montreal in 1642.

Most of the French settled in the St. Lawrence Valley, in what is now the Canadian Province of Quebec. (This area is still a French-speaking island in the English-speaking ocean of North America.) Other, more adventuresome souls, however, journeyed west in search of fur. They traveled enormous distances by paddling down rivers and across lakes in fragile birchbark canoes. These hardy French explorers traveled as far as the Rocky Mountains and the Gulf of Mexico. They were often accompanied by priests, especially Jesuit missionaries, who took as their special apostolate the conversion of the Native Americans.

One American historian, George Bancroft, once said, "Not a river was entered or a cape turned, but a Jesuit led the way." That comment was obviously an exaggeration, but these French Jesuits did seem to be everywhere. One of the most famous was Jacques Marquette (1637–1675), who, together with the explorer Louis Jolliet (1645–1700), discovered the Mississippi River. Other Jesuits established their headquarters near Mackinac Island in the upper Great Lakes. From there they spread out across Michigan, Illinois, and Wisconsin. Another famous Jesuit was the martyr Saint Jean de Brébeuf, who worked among the Indians near Georgian Bay in Ontario. Still others spread the gospel among the Indians in Maine and upstate New York.

Martyrs and Pioneers

One of the most heroic figures in the whole history of North America was the martyr Saint Isaac Jogues. Jogues, a Jesuit missionary, tried to evangelize the fierce Iroquois Indians, who were mortal enemies of the French. The Iroquois captured Jogues and subjected him to frightful tortures, which included the mutilation of his fingers. With the help of friendly Dutch Protestants, Jogues escaped from his captors and made his way back to France. There he received a hero's welcome and even obtained special permission from the pope to celebrate Mass with the mangled stumps of his hands.

Saint Isaac Jogues, Martyrs' Shrine, Auriesville, New York

Father Jacques Marquette and Louis Jolliet descending the Mississippi River in 1673, engraving, 19th century

Jogues could have remained in France for the rest of his life, basking in his fame and celebrity. Instead he decided to return to North America and to work among the very Indians who had so mistreated him. On October 18, 1646, the Iroquois murdered him. Today there is a shrine in his memory in upstate New York. Isaac Jogues and the other Jesuit martyrs are honored as the *North American martyrs*.

An interesting aspect of Catholic life in French America was the role played by women. In the Spanish empire women religious were almost exclusively cloistered nuns like Saint Rose of Lima (1586–1617). However, in French America women were pioneers in combining a life of prayer with teaching and nursing. Marie of the Incarnation (1599–1672), a saintly Ursuline nun, is known as the first woman missionary to the New World. Jeanne Mance (1606–1673), a nurse, established the first hospital in Montreal. Marguerite Bourgeoys (1620–1700) founded the Congregation de Notre Dame de Montreal, who opened schools for both French and Indian children.

CATHOLIC ID

Many places in the United States are named after saints. For example, cities in California are named San Francisco, San Diego, and Santa Barbara. Los Angeles was originally Nuestra Señora de los Angeles ("Our Lady of the Angels"). There is the beautiful city of Santa Fe ("Holy Faith") in New Mexico. Southern Maryland has St. Mary's City and St. Inigoes (Saint Ignatius). St. Paul and St. Louis are major cities on the Mississippi River. The reason that these places and many others are named after saints is that Catholics got there first. They chose those names in honor of saints whom they venerated back in their homelands.

In 1763 the French lost their North American empire to the British. Despite this political reversal the French maintained a strong identity in Quebec, as they do to this day. But elsewhere the story was different. In 1783, after the American Revolution, the whole area east of the Mississippi became part of the new American Republic. As American pioneers crossed the Appalachian Mountains and settled in the rich farmlands of the Midwest, they overwhelmed the tiny French population. Soon all that remained were place names to remind Americans that the French were the original pioneers in the Midwest.

The one exception in the United States was Louisiana, which retained a strong French identity. In 1803 Napoleon sold the vast Louisiana Territory to the United States for the bargain price of fifteen million dollars. The territory included a huge tract of land between the Mississippi River and the Rocky Mountains, and with its purchase the size of the United States was doubled. Much of the region was wilderness, but it would soon be explored by Meriwether Lewis and William Clark.

Marie of the Incarnation, first woman missionary to the New World

Are there any traces of the work of Catholic missionaries in the area where you live? What do you know about them?

143

Catholics in the Colonies

Both Spain and France were great Catholic powers, and so it is not surprising that they helped to spread the Catholic faith in the New World. What is surprising, however, is that Protestant England also played a role in bringing Catholicism to America.

You may recall that George Calvert, the first Lord Baltimore, obtained a charter from King Charles I of England that led in 1634 to the establishment of Maryland, a colony where Catholics and Protestants lived in peace with one another for a while. After the Revolution of 1688 in England, however, Catholics in Maryland were deprived of religious freedom and had to practice their religion privately. In New York, too, a brief period of religious toleration for Catholics came to an abrupt end in 1688. For almost a hundred years thereafter, the only place in the thirteen colonies where Catholics enjoyed religious freedom was Pennsylvania, thanks to the tolerance of Quakers who had founded the colony.

THEN & NOW

In 1791, thanks to the help of French Sulpician priests, Bishop John Carroll was able to open the first training school for priests in the United States. It was St. Mary's Seminary in Baltimore, and it still exists today.

At the time of the American Revolution, American Catholics faced a painful decision. Neither the British nor the leading patriots were at all friendly to them. One could hardly have blamed the Catholics if they had decided to remain neutral during the Revolution. Instead almost all the prominent Catholics sided with the patriot cause and supported the Revolution.

Once the United States secured its independence from England in 1783, the American Catholics reaped the reward of having supported the winning side. In all thirteen states they shared in the full religious freedom that was granted to everyone. Prejudice against Catholics seemed to vanish overnight.

Bishop John Carroll

The total number of American Catholics was still extremely small, about twenty-five thousand, or a mere one percent of the total population. But in 1784 Pope Pius VI began to organize the infant Church in America by choosing Father John Carroll (1735–1815) to be the "Superior of the Mission." Carroll, who came from an old Maryland Catholic family, proved to be an excellent choice. A few years later the American priests asked the pope to make

John Carroll, first Roman Catholic American archbishop, helped to establish the oldest Catholic college in the United States.

Carroll a bishop, and Pius VI agreed. On August 15, 1790, in the chapel of a castle in England, John Carroll was ordained the first bishop of Baltimore. His diocese included the whole United States. And for the next twenty-five years, Carroll led the Catholic Church in the United States with wisdom and foresight.

Carroll and American Catholics were not used to living in a free land. He had no previous experience to draw upon for guidance. In Europe either Catholics had enjoyed special favors from the government in Catholic countries such as Spain and France, or they had been persecuted by the government in Protestant countries such as England. Now, in the United States of America, Catholics were free. The government did not favor them, and it did not make life difficult for them. John Carroll thought that it was the ideal arrangement, and so did most American Catholics.

Bishop Carroll knew that the future always belongs to the young. For that reason he took a deep interest in Catholic education. He used money that he brought back with him from England to help to establish Georgetown College, the oldest Catholic college in the United States. In 1811 John Carroll was elevated to archbishop of Baltimore. When he died in 1815, the number of American Catholics was still modest, between 100,000 and 150,000, but Carroll had done his work well.

Elizabeth Ann Seton

In 1808 a young widow and recent convert to Catholicism arrived in Baltimore and opened a little elementary school. Her name was Elizabeth Ann Seton (1774–1821). Two years later she moved to Emmitsburg, Maryland, and there founded the American Sisters of Charity, a community that would eventually provide teachers for thousands of parochial schools across the country. Elizabeth Seton was canonized in 1975, the first native-born American to be so honored by the Church.

The number of women religious continued to grow throughout the nineteenth and early twentieth centuries. By 1963, when their numbers peaked, there were 177,000 women religious in the United States. They served the Church as teachers, nurses, missionaries, and social workers and in many other capacities. In the "man's world" of the nineteenth century, some nuns and sisters who headed large colleges and hospitals exercised more authority than any other women in American society at that time. Their contribution to American Catholicism was beyond measure.

 Do you agree with John Carroll, who believed that the future of Catholicism belongs to the young? Why?

Above: Saint Elizabeth Ann Seton, Dawley

Sister Maryanne, Sister of Charity, a volunteer at Camp Fatima, which provides programs for children and teens with special needs

145

The Immigrant Church

The year that John Carroll died, 1815, also marked the end of the wars of the French Revolution in Europe. For the first time in over two decades, it was fairly safe to travel across the Atlantic. As a result many Europeans began to emigrate to America in search of a better life. Most of them came from the British Isles and Germany. At first the number of immigrants was only a trickle, but it soon grew to be a flood.

This flow of immigrants led to an enormous increase in the Catholic population. By 1850 there were two million Catholics in the United States, which made them the largest religious denomination in the country. A mere fifteen years later, at the end of the Civil War, the Catholic population had doubled again to four million.

The American Catholic bishops had to provide churches and priests for these immigrants. In the case of the Germans, there was a demand for priests who could speak their language. There was also a pressing need for Catholic institutions such as schools, hospitals, and orphanages. Although many of the immigrants were very poor, they were amazingly generous to the Church. Many of them regarded

their Catholic faith as their most precious possession. They made huge sacrifices to build churches and schools so that they could hand on their religion to their children.

Many native-born Protestant Americans were alarmed by these immigrants, however. They pointed to the poverty of the Irish and the "foreignness" of the Germans as evidence that these Catholic newcomers would never make good citizens. The result was a revival of anti-Catholic bigotry, which had all but disappeared during the era of the American Revolution. Sometimes this anti-Catholic sentiment turned violent. In 1834 a mob burned an Ursuline convent near Boston. In 1844 "nativist" riots in Philadelphia led to the destruction of three Catholic churches and the death of a dozen people.

This wave of anti-Catholic bigotry reached its peak in the 1850s with the *Know-Nothings*. That was the popular name for a new political party that whipped up prejudice against Catholics and other "foreigners." A young lawyer in Illinois named Abraham Lincoln felt ashamed of his country when he saw how many Americans were voting for the Know-Nothings. Fortunately the Know-Nothings soon fell apart. This experience was frightening for American Catholics and reminded them how easily they could become targets for bigotry.

Church Leaders

In the early nineteenth century, not only were most Catholics immigrants, but so were their leaders, the bishops. Many were French, often refugees from the French Revolution. One of these men was Benedict Joseph Flaget (1763–1850), first bishop of Bardstown, Kentucky. His first cathedral was a log cabin in the wilderness. Another French-born bishop was Jean Baptiste Lamy (1814–1888), first archbishop of Santa Fe. His diocese originally included all of New Mexico, Colorado, Utah, and Arizona.

Irish immigrants also provided important bishops for the young American Church. One of the most capable was John England (1786–1842), first bishop of Charleston, South Carolina. Although his diocese was one of the smallest and poorest in the world, he became a national figure because of his innovative leadership. He wrote a constitution for his diocese that gave laypeople specific responsibilities. He also established the first American Catholic newspaper, started his own seminary, opened a school for African Americans, and persuaded the American bishops to meet regularly to discuss national issues.

Probably the most famous bishop of the era was John Hughes (1797–1864), fourth bishop and first archbishop of New York. Hughes was an Irish immigrant who came to this country as an unskilled laborer, and he had personal experience of poverty and prejudice. A tough and fearless leader, he could at times be headstrong and stubborn. But he was loved by his largely Irish flock because of the way that he defended them against their foes. This unity of bishops, priests, and people, which John Hughes exemplified so well, was to be one of the great strengths of the Catholic Church in the United States.

Pray that our country will continue to be blessed with strong Catholic leaders.

View of New York City, with St. Patrick's Cathedral in background, late 19th century

147

things to think about

How does knowing about the history of the Church in America help modern Catholics of different cultures to build stronger ties with one another?

Where do you think Isaac Jogues and other martyrs got the strength to be strong witnesses for their faith?

things to share

How would you explain to someone that American Catholics welcomed the American Revolution?

Knowing the history of our immigrant Church, how do you think we should treat today's immigrants to America?

WORDS TO REMEMBER

Find and define the following:

North American martyrs _____
_____
_____

Know-Nothings _____
_____
_____

OnLine WITH THE PARISH

Every parish belongs to a diocese. What is the name of your diocese? When was it first established, and who was its first bishop?

1 — Who was Junípero Serra, and why are he and other friars controversial figures today?

2 — What role did women play in the religious history of the French in North America?

3 — Why did anti-Catholic bigotry disappear during the American Revolution?

4 — Why was there a new wave of anti-Catholic bigotry in the early nineteenth century?

5 — Who was Archbishop John Hughes, and why was he so popular with the Catholics of New York?

Life in the Spirit

Immigrants to the United States have often been given an unpleasant reception by people who felt threatened by strangers. It happened to the Irish and Germans 150 years ago; it happened to the Italians and Poles 100 years ago. And it is happening now to America's most recent immigrants, Hispanics and Asians. American Catholics can take the lead in welcoming immigrants to our country. Pray, "Lord, we are all pilgrims and strangers in this world. Help us to work together to build up your kingdom on earth."

CHAPTER 13

THE CHURCH IN MODERN AMERICA
A.D. 1861–PRESENT

From age to age you gather a people to yourself, so that from east to west a perfect offering may be made to the glory of your name.

Eucharistic Prayer III

Immigrants getting off the Ellis Island ferry, New York City, 1900s

Have you ever had to take sides in a disagreement?
What was the result of your action?
Why do you think it is difficult to take sides?

The Civil War and Catholics

For reasons that we are still exploring today, a civil war tore apart the United States in the middle of the nineteenth century. At the heart of it was the question of human slavery. When the Civil War broke out in 1861, the country was divided between North and South. Like other Americans, Catholics were divided in their loyalties. As you might expect, Southern Catholics usually backed the Confederacy, and Northerners generally supported the Union. Catholic priests served as chaplains in both the Union and the Confederate armies.

In 1866, one year after the war ended, the American bishops met in Baltimore to discuss the state of the Catholic Church in America. Archbishop Martin Spalding (1810–1872) of Baltimore, who had once been a slave owner, pointed out that there were now four million freed blacks in the United States. Many had no religion and would have welcomed an invitation to become Catholics. Spalding wanted the Catholic Church to make a major effort to evangelize these emancipated slaves. "It is a golden opportunity," he said, "which, if neglected, may never come again."

Sadly, few of the other bishops showed much interest in the proposal, and Spalding's words turned out to be prophetic.

One reason why the bishops turned a deaf ear to Spalding's plea was that they had their hands full trying to care for the millions of Catholic immigrants who were streaming into the country. In the first two decades after the Civil War, immigration from Germany was especially heavy. Cities such as Milwaukee, St. Louis, and Cincinnati soon had flourishing German Catholic parishes. Some rural counties in the Midwest were dotted with German Catholic farming communities.

Immigrants at Ellis Island, Statue of Liberty in background, 1900s

Then, in the 1880s, another wave of immigrants arrived in America, and many of them were Catholics. These newcomers were from southern and eastern Europe and included Italians, Hungarians, Lithuanians, and a variety of Slavic peoples—Poles, Slovaks, Czechs, Slovenes, Croats, Ruthenians, and Ukrainians. Not all the new immigrants came from Europe, however. There were also Mexicans who came to work on the farms and railroads in the American Southwest. At the other end of the country, many French Canadians traveled south from rural Quebec to find work in the textile mills of New England.

One should not forget to mention the Catholics whose ancestors came to North America long before everyone else, the Native Americans. The nineteenth century was a sad time for them and a shameful one for the Europeans who drove them from their ancestral lands and herded them into reservations. However, Catholic missionaries were active on many of the reservations, opening churches and schools.

The Ruthenian and Ukrainian immigrants added a whole new dimension to American Catholicism. They were Byzantine Catholics who had their own distinctive religious traditions. They used Old Slavonic rather than Latin in their liturgy, they topped their churches with onion-shaped domes rather than steeples, and their priests were usually married men with families. In Europe these Byzantine Catholics had their own bishops who understood their customs. In America, however, they came under the authority of the local bishop in the place where they lived. Many of these bishops were horrified at the thought of married priests and banned them from their dioceses. In protest and desperation some 225,000 Byzantine Catholics left the Catholic Church and joined the Russian Orthodox Church in America.

The new immigrants made the Catholic Church in the United States more truly "catholic" than ever before. They also provoked another wave of anti-Catholic bigotry, spearheaded by the American Protective Association (APA). Members of this organization promised not to vote for Catholics, not to hire Catholics, not even to participate in strikes with them. Like other anti-Catholic organizations before and since, the APA enjoyed a brief moment of attention and then faded from the scene.

Labor riot at Haymarket Square, Chicago, May 4, 1886

The In-between Times

In the nineteenth century America was affected by the horrors of the Civil War. In the twentieth century profound changes would occur, especially because of two world wars. But the history of the Church in America is more than the story of wars. It is also the story of what goes on in between. Let's take a look at these in-between times.

The late nineteenth century in the United States is sometimes called the Gilded Age. During those decades the United States became the leading industrial country in the world. A few Americans became fabulously rich and then paraded their wealth for all to see in the form of lavish mansions, fancy country estates, and private railroad cars and yachts. It was a glorious time to be rich in America. There were few government regulations and even fewer labor unions. There was no income tax or minimum wage. Businessmen could run their factories, mines, and railroads pretty much as they pleased.

The people who paid the price for this state of affairs were, of course, the workers. Many of them toiled for long hours at low wages, often under terrible conditions. Women and children were especially exploited because they could be employed more cheaply than men. In the 1880s American workers reacted by organizing the first large and effective labor union, the Knights of Labor. Many of the union's members were Catholics, and this brought the organization to the attention of the American bishops.

Some of the bishops feared that the Knights of Labor was a dangerously radical organization, and they did not want Catholics to belong to it. This issue created a major crisis in American Catholic history. If the Church had forbidden American Catholic workers to join the union, it would have had a devastating effect on them. They would have concluded that the Church had sided with the rich, and they would have left the Church.

Three American Catholic bishops deserve great credit for preventing that from happening in America. They were James Cardinal Gibbons (1834–1921) of Baltimore, Archbishop John Ireland (1838–1918) of St. Paul, and Bishop John Keane (1839–1918), first rector of the Catholic University of America. They argued that workers had a right to form labor unions such as the Knights of Labor. Only a few years later, in 1891, Pope Leo XIII said so explicitly in his encyclical *Rerum Novarum*.

CATHOLIC ID Another person who shared an optimistic point of view about Catholics in the United States was Father Isaac Hecker (1819–1888), a convert to Catholicism and the founder of the Paulists. Hecker believed that the United States was ripe for evangelization because America and Catholicism had so much in common. He liked to think of himself as a missionary who would explain the Catholic faith to America and America to the Church. The members of his community are still active in evangelization today.

Secret meetings were held to organize workers and explain union benefits.

Americanism

Another issue split the American bishops at this time. That issue was a long-standing division between those who might be called the optimists and those who might be called the pessimists.

The optimists were headed by Archbishop John Ireland, a dynamic go-getter who was sometimes called the "consecrated blizzard of the Northwest." A deeply patriotic man, Archbishop Ireland believed that the American system of democracy and religious freedom provided an ideal setting for the Catholic Church to thrive and flourish. Ireland welcomed contacts with non-Catholics, tried to bridge the gap between public and parochial schools, and urged Catholic immigrants to become thoroughly American as soon as possible.

Pope Leo XIII

The pessimists, headed by Archbishop Michael Corrigan (1839–1902) of New York, had their doubts about the readiness of Americans to become Catholic. They were concerned about preserving Catholic identity in overwhelmingly Protestant America. For that reason they told Catholic immigrants to hold on to their ancestral traditions and discouraged contacts with Protestants. They

also strongly supported parochial schools as a way of handing on the Catholic faith.

Pope Leo XIII took a close interest in the Catholic Church in America. In 1895 he warned American Catholics not to turn their Church into something different from the Catholic Church in the rest of the world. In 1899 he repeated this warning in a famous public letter to Cardinal Gibbons. This led some people to say that the Holy Father had condemned "Americanism."

In reply Cardinal Gibbons assured the pope that no American Catholics held the views that he condemned. He explained to the Holy Father that American Catholics wanted their Church to be thoroughly at home in America. But, he said, they were also loyal Catholics who would never endanger the unity of the Church or water down the faith to make it seem more attractive to non-Catholics. In 1902, just a year before the end of his long life, the pontiff wrote again to the American bishops. This time he told them how pleased he was with the Church in the United States.

 Do you think it is hard or easy to be a Catholic in the United States? Why?

155

Maryknoll missionary working with Guatemalan women

Coming of Age

In 1908 Rome officially recognized that the United States was no longer a mission country. Three years later two American priests founded the Catholic Foreign Mission Society of America, better known as Maryknoll. After centuries of benefiting from the services of European missionaries, the United States now began to repay the debt by sending American priests, brothers, and sisters to the four corners of the world.

The early twentieth century was a golden time for big-city parishes in the United States. In places such as Boston, New York, Philadelphia, Chicago, St. Louis, and Milwaukee, there were solidly Catholic neighborhoods at the center of which was the local parish church. Some of these parishes contained as many as twenty thousand or thirty thousand Catholics. People commonly spoke of the "parish plant," meaning a complex of buildings that might occupy a whole square block and include a church, rectory, convent, parish hall, one or more parochial schools, perhaps even a high school, gymnasium, and parish center.

Before the days of automobiles and television, these parish plants were often busy day and night. They were social as well as religious centers. They provided all kinds of parish societies for both men and women, athletic teams and marching bands for young people, and sometimes even drama clubs. In a typical parish there was a never-ending round of dances, picnics, concerts, plays, card games, and in the summer, boat rides and bus trips to shrines and resorts. The parish was so much a part of people's lives that they would identify the area of the city where they lived, not by the name of the street or neighborhood, but by the name of the local parish church.

Loyalties were especially strong in *national parishes,* which cared for the needs of one particular ethnic group, such as the Poles or the Italians. By the 1920s there were thousands of these national parishes scattered across the United States. In Chicago alone in 1916 there were 122 national parishes serving 15 different ethnic groups. These parishes served a great purpose as way stations where immigrants could feel at home in a strange new land. There people could meet, hear their native language spoken in the pulpit, and carry on the special religious traditions that had been brought from the old country.

Then & Now

In 1922 a new law in the state of Oregon required parents to send their children to public schools. In effect it made all private and religious schools illegal. Catholics were shocked at the unfairness of this law, so were many Protestants, Jews, and unbelievers. They all feared that it might spread to other states. The Catholic bishops took the lead in fighting this law, and in 1925 the U.S. Supreme Court declared it illegal. No one has ever again questioned the right of parents to send their children to schools of their choice.

After World War I

Those who study world history know the importance of World War I. For the first time the entire world waged war. Millions were killed far from home by the new technological weapons of the age. It was to be the "war to end all wars."

After World War I there was a reaction against America's involvement in world affairs and a resentment of foreigners in America. Harsh new laws limited the number of immigrants who could come to the United States from southern and eastern Europe. Everyone knew that these laws were aimed mainly at Catholics and Jews.

Alfred E. Smith, first Catholic to be nominated for president of the U.S., 1928

The 1920s witnessed the emergence and growth of a powerful new secret society, the *Ku Klux Klan.* Members of the Klan dressed in white sheets and hoods to conceal their identity. They liked to show off their strength and frighten people by organizing parades in many American cities, including the nation's capital. The Klan was anti-Jewish, anti-black, and especially, anti-Catholic. For a brief period in the 1920s, it was a powerful political force.

Ku Klux Klan members chanting during cross burning

In 1928, for the first time in American history, a major political party nominated a Catholic for president of the United States. His name was Alfred E. Smith. As governor of New York State, Smith had won wide respect. But when he ran for president on the Democratic ticket, he touched off another round of anti-Catholic bigotry. A whispering campaign spread rumors that the pope would take over the country if Smith were elected president. In fact a photo of Governor Smith at the dedication of a tunnel in New York City was circulated in some Protestant churches in the South. People were told that it was a tunnel under the Atlantic Ocean to Rome and that the pope would use it to come to Washington once Smith was elected.

Smith was badly defeated by Herbert Hoover in the election, at least partly because of his religion. It was an indication that there was still a fear of Catholics in the United States. However, American Catholics kept their sense of humor. They told the story that after the election Al Smith sent a one-word telegram to the pope. It read, "Unpack!"

 How do you identify yourself as a Catholic today?

New York City soup kitchen during the Great Depression, 1931

Catholics and the Depression

In the 1930s all Americans were affected by the Great Depression, which left millions unemployed and many others living on the edge of poverty. Several American Catholics attracted widespread attention when they suggested solutions for America's social problems.

One of them was a priest named Charles Coughlin (1891–1979), an electrifying speaker who was one of the first people in America to use the radio to spread his message. On Sunday afternoons millions of people across the country dropped everything to listen to Father Coughlin's broadcasts from his Shrine of the Little Flower in Royal Oak, Michigan. He was persuasive in describing the problems of the day, but he had few real solutions. Before long he was lashing out wildly at President Franklin Roosevelt, capitalists, communists, Jews, and international bankers, blaming them for the country's economic troubles. During World War II he became so offensive that his bishop, under pressure from the U.S. government, finally forced him off the air.

A very different sort of person was Dorothy Day (1897–1980), a convert to Catholicism from communism. In 1933, together with her friend Peter Maurin (1877–1949), she began the Catholic Worker movement, which called for radical changes in America's economic system. Dorothy Day also opened shelters for the poor and homeless—"houses of hospitality" she called them. She lived with the poor and ministered to them.

World War II and After

During World War II (1939–1945), millions of Catholics served in the armed forces. A familiar figure to many of them was Francis Cardinal Spellman (1889–1967) of New York, who was also the military bishop and traveled all over the world to visit American troops on active duty. Another popular figure was Bishop Fulton J. Sheen (1895–1979), a dramatic public speaker who attracted a national audience of millions, first on radio and later on television. Both Cardinal Spellman and Bishop Sheen were outspoken foes of communism during the height of the Cold War between the United States and the Soviet Union.

The postwar years were a period of amazing growth for the Catholic Church in the United States. Between 1940 and 1960 the Catholic population doubled from twenty-one million to forty-two million. Catholics were better off economically than they had ever been before. Many veterans took advantage of government loans to become the first members of their families to attend college. Like many other successful Americans, millions of Catholics moved to the suburbs. In the 1950s Catholic schools, seminaries, and novitiates were filled to capacity. New churches were erected at a dizzying rate. Never before had American Catholics felt more secure.

In the late 1960s and 1970s, however, American Catholicism experienced a major crisis. Within a few years Sunday Mass attendance dropped sharply, Catholic school enrollment declined, and vocations to the priesthood and religious life fell at an alarming rate. For the first time in history, large numbers of priests left the active ministry, and many brothers and sisters returned to lay life. Many American Catholics were bewildered and wondered what was happening to their Church.

Historians still argue about the reasons for this crisis. Some blame the unsettling impact of the Second Vatican Council, which introduced changes for which many were largely unprepared. Others point to the great upsets that took place in American society at that time, such as the Vietnam War and the civil rights movement. Still others mention the social changes in the American Catholic community itself. Many American Catholics now lived in sprawling middle-class

suburbs rather than in close-knit city neighborhoods. They no longer felt the strong sense of Catholic identity that their parents and grandparents had enjoyed.

All these factors probably played some role in the crisis that the Catholic Church in the United States experienced at that time. It was so serious that some friendly Protestant observers wondered if the Catholic Church was actually going to fall apart and disappear. Needless to say, that did not happen. Many times in its long history, the Church has sprung back stronger than ever after a major crisis. It is not so surprising, therefore, that the Catholic Church in the United States survived the crisis of the 1960s and 1970s. There were bumps and bruises, to be sure, but it did survive to proclaim the gospel to a new generation of Americans.

 See how far back you can trace your Catholic roots in America.

Bishop Fulton J. Sheen, an extremely popular Catholic radio and television speaker in America, reached millions from the 1930s to the 1950s

things to think about

Why would it have been a disaster for the Church if the bishops had forbidden Catholics to become members of the Knights of Labor?

Why were American Catholics surprised when they were confronted by a major crisis in their ranks in the 1960s and 1970s?

things to share

How can we show that we are both loyal citizens and faithful members of the Catholic Church? Name as many ways as you can.

If someone says to you that Catholics have never been the victims of bigotry and prejudice in the United States, what would you say?

WORDS TO REMEMBER

Find and define the following:

national parishes _____

_____

_____

Ku Klux Klan _____

_____

_____

OnLine

WITH THE PARISH

The parish is the most important point of contact between the Church and individual Catholics. How would you compare your parish today with the big-city parishes of the early twentieth century? In what ways does your parish still resemble one of those parishes? In what ways is it different? Why?

Testing 1, 2, 3

How did James Cardinal Gibbons of Baltimore explain to Pope Leo XIII that the Catholic Church had nothing to fear from genuine "Americanism"?

1

Why was the establishment of Maryknoll a sign of the coming of age of American Catholicism?

2

In the early twentieth century, what did American Catholics mean when they spoke of the "parish plant"?

3

What were some examples of anti-Catholic bigotry in the United States in the 1920s?

4

Why did so many Byzantine Catholics join the Russian Orthodox Church in America during this period of history?

5

Life in the Spirit

Dorothy Day was one of the most remarkable American Catholics of the twentieth century. Her influence did not come from any position of authority that she held. Rather, it came from her love of the poor and her personal service to them. She also spent a lot of time every day in prayer. What does that tell you about the connection between prayer and helping others?

161

CHAPTER 14

THE TWENTIETH CENTURY AND BEYOND

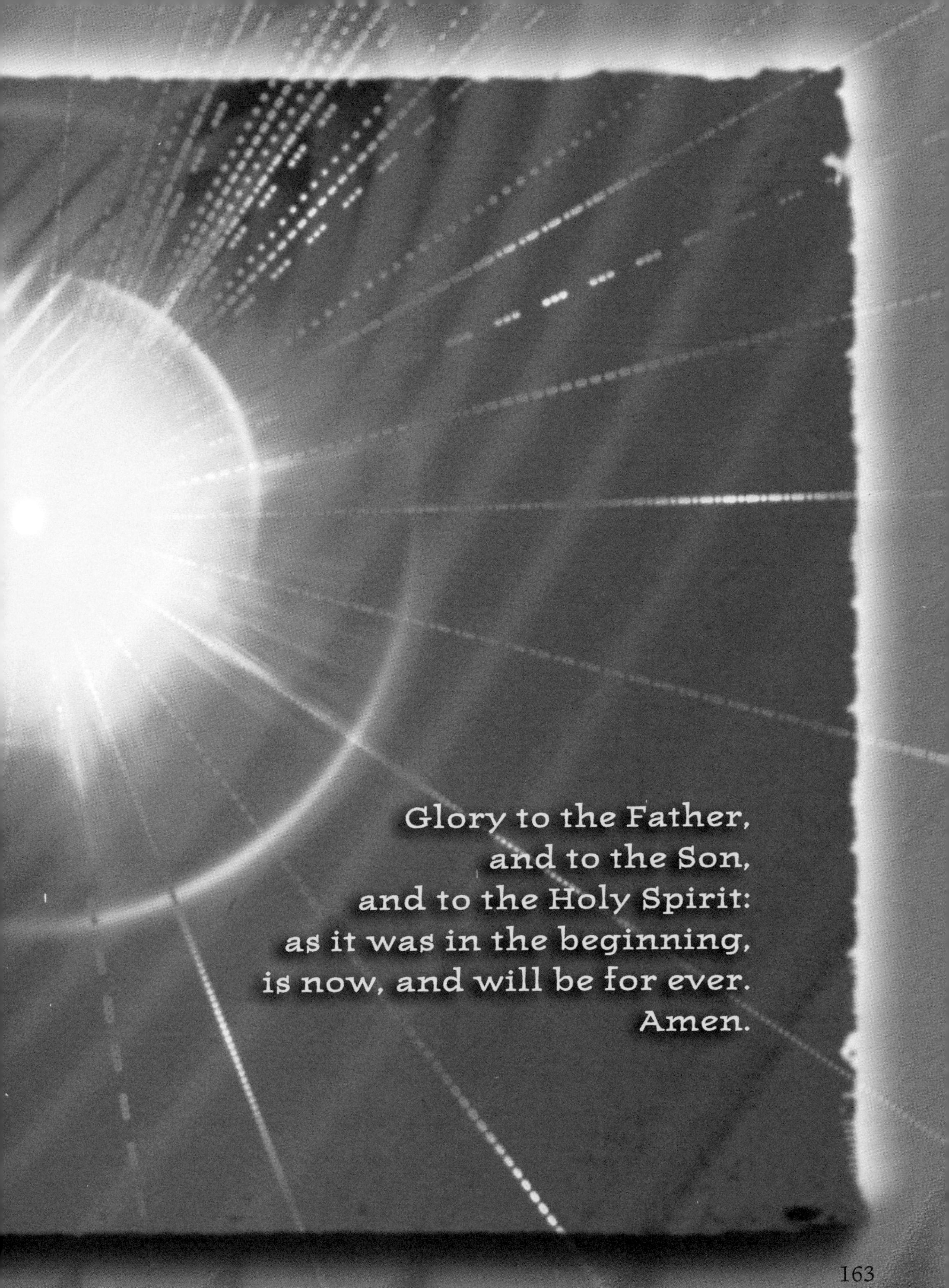

Glory to the Father,
and to the Son,
and to the Holy Spirit:
as it was in the beginning,
is now, and will be for ever.
Amen.

Nazi concentration camp, Auschwitz, Poland

Most people say that we need distance
from an experience in order to see it
more clearly. What do you think?

Trial and Triumph

We now turn to the most recent period of Church history. In many ways it has been a time of trial because of war and persecution. It has been frightening because of the nuclear age. But it also has been exciting, especially because of the Second Vatican Council (1962–1965) and the Church renewal that followed it.

Most people would agree that the Second Vatican Council was the most important event in the history of the Catholic Church in the twentieth century. Both Pope John XXIII, who summoned the council, and Pope Paul VI, who brought it to a conclusion, played key roles in its success. But both pontiffs were building on the achievements of the earlier popes of the twentieth century.

Pope Pius X was the first pope elected in the twentieth century. He died at the outbreak of World War I, the bloodiest conflict that the world had yet witnessed. His successor was Pope Benedict XV

(1914–1922). Benedict is sometimes called "the forgotten pope" because his pontificate was overshadowed by the war years. He was horrified by the war, warning that it would be "the death of civilized Europe." On several occasions he tried to bring the war to an end by urging both sides to lay down their arms.

Neither side was pleased with Benedict's appeal for peace. Both sides wanted victory, not peace. Today Benedict appears to have been far wiser than the statesmen of that era. If they had heeded his appeal for peace, they might have saved millions of lives and prevented such catastrophes as the Communist Revolution in Russia in 1917 and, later, the rise to power of the Nazis in Germany.

Benedict's successor was Pope Pius XI (1922–1939), who had spent most of his life as a librarian. If anyone expected him to be a shy leader, they received a big surprise. Pius XI soon showed himself to be a

Mussolini and Hitler

most serious criticism that Hitler had received from any world leader up to that time. The encyclical was smuggled into Germany under the nose of the Gestapo (the secret police) and read from the pulpits of 11,500 churches on Palm Sunday in 1937.

The following year, as Hitler stepped up his persecution of Jews in Germany, Pius XI made a public statement: "It is impossible for a Christian to take part in anti-Semitism. . . . Through Christ and in Christ we are the spiritual progeny of Abraham. Spiritually we are all Semites [Jews]." Even earlier, in 1925, he gave the Church the new feast of Christ the King as a way of reminding Catholics that their first loyalty must be to Jesus Christ, not to any dictator like Hitler or Mussolini.

 How can we help to rid the world of racist ideas?

lion, which was exactly the kind of leader that the Church needed at that time. In Europe it was the age of the dictators—Mussolini in Italy, Stalin in Russia, and Hitler in Germany.

In dealing with these dictators and with other states, Pius XI acted on two levels: He tried to negotiate treaties or concordats with them, not for the purpose of friendship, but to obtain rights for the Church. But he also spoke directly to the Catholic people of the world through a series of important encyclicals.

Pius XI's treatment of Nazi Germany is a good example of his style of leadership. Shortly after Adolf Hitler came to power in 1933, Pius XI signed a concordat with the Third Reich. However, Hitler violated the treaty almost from the day it was signed. He closed Catholic schools, disbanded Catholic youth organizations, and arrested any Catholics who dared to criticize him.

In 1937 the pope responded by addressing the Catholics of Germany in a German-language encyclical. He did not denounce Hitler's regime as such, but he did criticize the violation of the rights of Catholics and the racism of the Nazis. It was the

Pope John Paul II with former prisoners of Nazi concentration camps

War and Its Aftermath

When Pope Pius XI died in February 1939 and the cardinals met to select his successor, everyone feared that another war was about to break out in Europe. For that reason the cardinals picked Eugenio Pacelli, who took the name of Pius XII (1939–1958). He had spent his whole life as a papal diplomat and had been the right-hand man of Pope Pius XI. He seemed to be the ideal pope to guide the Church through the coming storm.

World War II, which began on September 1, 1939, was even more horrible than World War I and cost some forty million lives. Many of the casualties were civilians, victims of the bombing of cities by both sides.

Pius XII's role in World War II has been the subject of much debate. He has been criticized for not issuing stronger public denunciations of Nazi war crimes, especially the Holocaust, Hitler's effort to wipe out the Jews of Europe. In fact Pius XII did criticize the Nazis several times, most notably in his 1942 Christmas radio broadcast. For the most part, however, following the diplomatic habits of a lifetime, he preferred to work behind the scenes to relieve the sufferings of the victims

of war. After the war, many people, especially Jews, thanked him for his efforts on their behalf.

At the end of World War II, in 1945, Europe was a divided continent. Winston Churchill, the wartime British prime minister, said that an "Iron Curtain" had descended on Europe, splitting it into a Western half that was free and an Eastern half that was under communist rule.

In Eastern Europe the communists subjected the Catholic Church to severe persecution. Church buildings and Catholic schools were closed; priests were jailed; religious orders were outlawed; lay Catholics were barred from public life. The leading Catholic churchmen were arrested, convicted of "treason" at rigged trials, and sentenced to long prison terms. Their names became well known in the West—for example, Aloysius Cardinal Stepinac in Yugoslavia, Joseph Cardinal Mindszenty in Hungary, and Archbishop Joseph Beran in

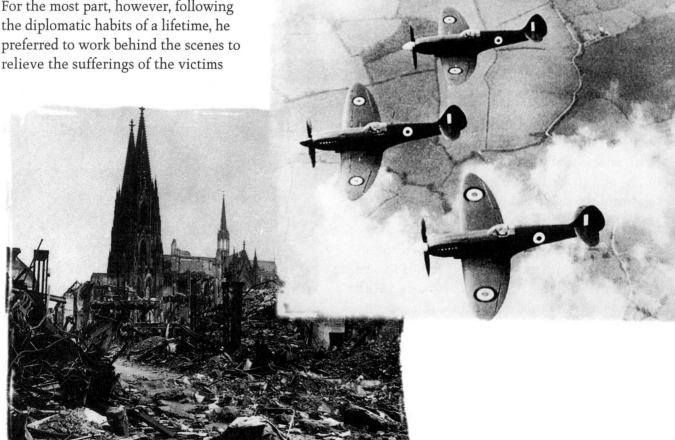

Ruins around the cathedral in Cologne

Maryknoll Bishop Walsh after his release from a Chinese prison

Czechoslovakia. In Poland Stephen Cardinal Wyszynski was placed under house arrest.

In two European countries the persecution was especially brutal. In Albania a fanatical regime declared the country an atheistic state and outlawed the practice of all religion. In Ukraine, then a part of the Soviet Union, the Soviet dictator, Joseph Stalin, an atheist, forced the Ukrainian Catholic Church to become part of the Orthodox Church. He also exiled all the Catholic bishops to Siberia. And in China, after the communists came to power in 1949, they expelled all foreign missionaries and launched a bloody repression of the Church.

Since the collapse of the Soviet Union and the fall of the Iron Curtain in 1989, the memory of these bad old days has faded quickly. Some young people may find it hard to believe that such conditions existed in their lifetime. As Christians we must forgive our enemies. But we should not forget that terrible half century of persecution or overlook the high price that many Christians had to pay to be faithful to their religion.

Christian Democracy

In Western Europe it was a different story. The Catholic Church experienced an impressive revival after World War II. One of the clearest signs of this revival was the emergence of Christian Democratic parties in many countries. These were political parties founded under Catholic patronage to promote Christian values and principles in public life. The parties were Christian but not clerical. That is, they were led, not by the clergy, but by dedicated laypeople, many of whom took their inspiration from the teachings of popes such as Leo XIII and Pius XI.

Throughout the postwar decades the United States and its Western European allies were locked in a struggle with communism known as the Cold War. For that reason in 1949 the United States and most Western European countries formed a military alliance known as the North Atlantic Treaty Organization, or NATO. It was equally important for the countries of Western Europe to be able to offer their people an attractive alternative to communism, and they were able to do so thanks to the enlightened policies of the Christian Democrats.

What do you think was the greatest challenge Pope Pius XII had to face?

Catholics who understand the teachings of the Church know that anti-Semitism is a serious evil. The Second Vatican Council had this to say about all forms of discrimination: "With respect to the fundamental rights of the person, every type of discrimination, whether social or cultural, whether based on sex, race, color, social condition, language, or religion, is to be overcome and eradicated as contrary to God's intent" (*Church Today*, 29).

American Catholic bishop with sisters in Ghana, Africa

Asia and Africa

After World War II enormous changes took place in Asia and Africa. In the famous words of a British prime minister, "winds of change" ripped through the two continents in the 1950s and 1960s. These changes led to the end of the old European colonial empires and the emergence of dozens of new countries. Fortunately, in both Asia and Africa, the Catholic Church had put down deep roots and for several decades had been preparing local clergy and religious to take over Church leadership.

As far back as 1919, Pope Benedict XV told missionaries to encourage native vocations. Pius XI continued this policy. In 1926 he ordained six Chinese bishops in Rome, and in 1930 he appointed the first black African bishop, a native of Ethiopia. In 1939 Pius XII went a step further and, in a dramatic ceremony in Rome, ordained twelve bishops from all over the world, including two black African bishops. By the end of Vatican II in 1965, there were 160 Asian bishops, 68 African bishops, and thousands of native priests and religious. The Church was no longer European; it was Asian and African, too.

As often in the past, "the blood of martyrs has been the seed of Christians" in those two continents. In the African country of Uganda in 1886, thirty-three Catholic and Protestant converts were put to death by a cruel king when they resisted his immoral advances. More recently, in China and Vietnam, millions of Catholics have suffered for their faith under communist regimes. In the Sudan, Africa's largest country, a Muslim government has harassed the Christian minority.

Despite these difficulties, or perhaps because of them, the Christian population continues to grow. It is estimated that soon half of the population of Africa will be Christian. In Asia only about three percent of the people are Christian. But there, too, the Catholic Church has made amazing gains in Korea and also in the Philippines, which today is the third-largest Catholic country in the world.

Latin America

For many years the sleeping giant of the Catholic world was the Church in Latin America. The Church there suffered from terrible poverty, a severe shortage of priests, and a laity who often had received little religious instruction. Frequent revolutions and changes in governments also took a heavy toll on organized Catholic life. Even today conditions vary widely from prosperous countries such as Argentina and Chile to poor countries such as Bolivia and Paraguay. Sometimes vast differences exist within the same country. In the cities of Brazil and Venezuela, modern skyscrapers stand alongside dreadful slums and the shantytowns of the poor.

In 1899 Pope Leo XIII summoned all the bishops of Latin America to a meeting in Rome in the hope of bringing this sleeping giant to life. However, real progress did not come until decades later. In the 1950s the bishops of Latin America formed their own regional organization.

Many priests and religious became outspoken advocates of the poor and the oppressed. A few went to extremes and even joined violent guerrilla movements. Most, however, followed the example

Area of Rio de Janeiro, Brazil

of outstanding bishops such as Archbishop Helder Camara in Brazil, who became world famous as a champion of democracy and social justice. In El Salvador, on March 24, 1980, Archbishop Oscar Romero (1917–1980), an outspoken critic of the government, was murdered while celebrating Mass in his own cathedral.

Renewal came not only from above but also from below. In many villages and neighborhoods where there were no priests, small groups of laypeople began to meet regularly for prayer and reflection on the Scriptures. Today almost half the Catholics in the world live in Latin America. In fact Brazil and Mexico are the two largest Catholic countries.

During the war years, when many Catholics worked closely together with Protestants and Orthodox Christians, they came to appreciate the richness of these other Christian traditions. Such experiences gave Catholics an interest in promoting the unity of all Christians, a movement that is called *ecumenism*. By the late 1940s and early 1950s, winds of change were beginning to blow through the Church. More and more Catholics became interested in the study of the Bible, a deeper vision of the Church, a better appreciation of worship, and a desire for greater contacts with Christians of other traditions. It explains why many Catholics were ready for the Second Vatican Council in 1962.

 Why is it so important for the Church to be an advocate for the poor and the oppressed?

PERSONAL PROFILE

Each year we celebrate a feast in honor of some African martyrs referred to in this lesson. Many faithful Christians were killed in Uganda by King Mwanga during the years 1885 to 1887. Among these were Charles Lwanga and his companions. Without giving up their Catholic faith, these martyrs were put to death by the sword and by burning. Their feast day is June 3.

Young people participating in World Youth Day

Vatican II and After

After the death of Pope Pius XII in 1958, the cardinals elected one of the most beloved popes of this century, Angelo Roncalli, who took the name of John XXIII (1958–1963). When Pope John was elected, he was seventy-seven years old. Everyone expected him to be a "transitional" pope who would last only a few years and make no changes. He did live only five more years, but he had such an impact on the Church that historians sometimes speak of "Pope John's Revolution."

First of all, Pope John changed the way that people looked at the papacy. Pope Pius XII was a quiet, scholarly man born of wealthy parents. Pope John XXIII, the son of poor farmers, was a jovial and outgoing man who never lost the common touch. Everyone was impressed with his warmth and affection. He spoke often of social justice and peace, and the response was overwhelmingly favorable. When he died in 1963, he was mourned throughout the world as no pope had been mourned for centuries.

The most important decision of John XXIII was to summon an ecumenical council, the Second Vatican Council, which met in Rome for four sessions between October 11, 1962, and December 8, 1965. Over two thousand bishops were usually in attendance, and they discussed just about every aspect of Catholic faith and life. Despite efforts to impose secrecy on the council, the daily discussions of the bishops became worldwide news and were reported on television every evening.

The work of Vatican II can be summarized in two foreign words, one Italian and one French: *aggiornamento* and *ressourcement*. *Aggiornamento* meant bringing the Church up-to-date, making it relevant in the modern world. However, that did not mean abandoning the ancient faith handed down from the apostles or imitating every passing modern fad. That is where the second word, *ressourcement* comes in. It means "a return to the sources." That is how the bishops at Vatican II wanted to modernize the Church—not by slavishly imitating the secular world, but by going back to the sources of our faith. They wanted to go back to the Scriptures and to Jesus himself, to be sure that the Church was being faithful to him.

A good example of this process is the change that the council made in the liturgy, or public worship, of the Church. The bishops modernized the Mass by changing the language from Latin to the language of the people. In doing so, they were not turning their backs on tradition. Instead, they were returning to the oldest Catholic tradition. In addition to liturgical reforms, the ecumenical spirit that was so important at the council continues to guide the Church today in our relationships with our separated brothers and sisters in Christ and with people of other religions.

Pope John died shortly after the end of the first session of the Second Vatican Council. He was succeeded by Cardinal Montini, a leading figure in the council, who took the name of Paul VI (1963–1978). He guided the council to its conclusion on December 8, 1965, and then faced the difficult challenge of leading the Church through the turbulent years that followed.

Some Catholics resisted the decisions of Vatican II, fearful that they would endanger the integrity of the Catholic faith. Other critics wanted faster and more radical changes. Moreover, in the years immediately following the end of the council, the Church appeared to be in disorder. In many countries Mass attendance declined, vocations fell off, priests left the active ministry, and religious left their monasteries and convents. Many wondered whether the Catholic Church was falling apart. Some who had been strong supporters of change now drew back in fright.

It fell to Paul VI to lead the Church through these difficult years of the late 1960s and 1970s. He faced the challenges of his pontificate with faith and courage. In doing so he demonstrated why Jesus gave us the papacy by preserving the unity of the Church and bringing the "bark of Peter" safely through these troubled waters. In 1978 he was succeeded by Pope John Paul I, whose pontificate lasted only thirty-four days. He in turn was succeeded by John Paul II, the first non-Italian pope in over four hundred years and the first Polish pope in the long history of the Church.

A Never–Ending Story

When will the history of the Church be completed? Not until the end of time. Jesus promised that the Church will last until he comes again. That is why we can say that the history of the Church is still being made—each and every day. And you are a part of that history. You have the choice of being a saint or a sinner, of making a positive contribution to the Church or not. Sometimes it is not an easy choice. But knowing the history of the Church and its highlights, you can be confident that God is still with the Church and that the Holy Spirit is guiding this community of faith so that it will be true to its divine founder, Jesus Christ.

 What, in your opinion, is the most interesting period of Church history and why?

There have been twenty-one ecumenical councils in the history of the Church:

Nicaea I (325)	Lateran IV (1215)
Constantinople I (381)	Lyons I (1245)
Ephesus (431)	Lyons II (1274)
Chalcedon (451)	Vienne (1311–1312)
Constantinople II (553)	Constance (1414–1418)
Constantinople III (680–681)	Florence (1438–1445)
Nicaea II (787)	Lateran V (1512–1517)
Constantinople IV (869–870)	Trent (1545–1563)
Lateran I (1123)	Vatican I (1869–1870)
Lateran II (1139)	Vatican II (1962–1965)
Lateran III (1179)	

PUTTING IT TOGETHER

things to think about

Pope John Paul II said that young people should know history because that knowledge can help them to be tolerant, understanding, and respectful in every situation. What do you think he meant?

Why was the Second Vatican Council so important?

things to share

What great changes did the Church in Africa and Asia experience during the 1950s and 1960s?

How would you help someone to see that the Church has tried to fight against tyrants during the past 150 years?

WORDS TO REMEMBER

Find and define the following:

aggiornamento _____

_____

_____

ressourcement _____

_____

_____

OnLine
WITH THE PARISH

How can you help other members of your parish to understand that they, too, are part of the history of the Church? Brainstorm ideas with your group.

How did Adolf Hitler go about persecuting the Church?

1

Describe how communists persecuted the Church in Eastern Europe.

2

Why was the Catholic Church in Latin America often regarded as a sleeping giant? How has it come to life in recent years?

3

How was Europe divided by the Iron Curtain after World War II? What effect did this have on the Church?

4

What great services did Pope Paul VI render to the Church during his pontificate?

5

Life in the Spirit

These words were used as part of the prayer of the council fathers at Vatican II. Make them your own today as you pray to God:

Be the guide of our actions, indicate the path we should take, and show us what we must do so that, with your help, our work may be in all things pleasing to you.

CHAPTER 15

THE STORY IN ART

May the favor of the Lord our God be ours.
Prosper the work of our hands!
Prosper the work of our hands!

Psalm 90:17

The work of an artist
"speaks to our capacity for
delight and wonder, to the sense of mystery
surrounding our lives: to our sense of pity,
and beauty, and pain."

Joseph Conrad

Art really can "speak" to us. It speaks of truly spiritual things, such as delight, wonder, mystery, and pain. Has your spirit ever been touched by art, by something in music or painting or sculpture?

The story of the Church is told in a powerful way through people and events. It is also told through the vision of artists. Let's take a look at what architecture, painting, sculpture, music, and drama have to tell us about the story of the Church and its journey in faith.

The Story in Architecture

One of the first things a faith community needs is a space in which to worship together. The first churches of the early Christians were their homes. But as the number of believers increased, especially after the Edict of Milan, larger spaces were needed. So church buildings were designed and constructed.

The designing and building of space for a specific use is called *architecture*.

As Christianity became the religion of the Roman Empire, old Roman basilicas (official buildings) were often converted into churches. New churches were built on the model of a basilica, adapted to the shape of a cross. What did a basilica look like?

In every basilica there was a large center *nave*, or assembly area, where the people gathered. The nave was sometimes divided by pillars to form side aisles. The nave ended in a domed area called an *apse*. This is where the altar was placed. The walls of the basilica were often covered with mosaics. *Mosaics* are images made by using colored stones or tiles.

As Christianity spread, new kinds of churches were designed and built. The architects drew on the engineering genius of the Romans, who were the first to use rounded arches and domes. The architects of Christian churches used these Roman domes and rounded arches, but they devised something new, too. They learned how to make a new kind of ceiling. Imagine a barrel placed on its side and then sliced in half. That is what the architects imagined. And they constructed it in stone. The result was a new architectural discovery: the *barrel vault*. Of course the walls had to be very thick and sturdy to support the weight of the arches, vaults, and dome.

Churches with all these Roman features were called *Romanesque*. A Romanesque church "feels" stable and strong. It reflects and expresses a faith that is rooted and sure.

Eastern Ideas

While church architects were experimenting in places such as Italy, France, and Germany, architects in the East followed a relatively consistent style. The style of the Eastern churches is called *Byzantine*, from "Byzantium," an old name for Constantinople. The interior of a Byzantine church is characterized by a large central dome. Often in large churches there are also several small domes, defining smaller spaces. In some areas of the East, the domes are onion-shaped. The inside walls are usually covered with mosaics of the Trinity, Jesus Christ as ruler of all, and Our Lady and the saints.

Now let's return to the West and continue to explore the changing art of church architecture.

Basilica of St. John Lateran, Rome, A.D. 315, showing barrel vault ceiling used later in Romanesque churches

Onion-shaped domes of St. Basil, Orthodox church, Moscow, now a museum

Gothic, Sainte Chapelle, Paris

Letting in the Light

The growth of towns and the rise of the first great universities in the twelfth century stirred a new artistic and intellectual spirit. Christian thinkers and artists emphasized their belief that the redeeming work of Christ touched all of creation. This meant that art, like the rest of creation, can lead us to God, our creator. Such thinking led these artists to produce vivid expressions of human life itself, full of beauty, vitality, joy, and hope. Because of Jesus, human beings are seen as redeemed, bathed in the light of God's love.

How were these insights and ideas reflected in architecture? Around 1120 architects developed a *ribbed* vault. In a ribbed vault arching and intersecting stone ribs support a vaulted ceiling made of thin stone panels; the weight of the stone is distributed through the ribs.

This discovery made it possible to open up the walls with large windows. All the arches of the vaults and windows, instead of being round, reached to a point. Additional stone supports called *flying buttresses* were attached to the walls on the outside. (Look at the picture of Notre Dame on page 62.) All these new developments—ribbed vaults, pointed arches, taller windows, and flying buttresses—resulted in churches that were soaring and full of light, drawing the eye and the heart upward in awe and hope.

Those who hated change named this style of architecture *Gothic* after the barbarian tribe of the Goths. It was a term of contempt. Soon, however, Gothic architecture spread all over Europe. And the style is still very popular today.

Baroque and Beautiful

Do you remember how the Church responded to the Protestant Reformation in the sixteenth century?

The Council of Trent (1545–1563) and the powerful movement of the Counter-Reformation were reflected not only in Church teaching but also in art. The new burst of Catholic life energized

Baroque, altar, Church of the Gesú, Rome

by this movement was celebrated in art that was elaborate, joyous, and dramatic. Again, critics gave the new movement an unflattering name. They called it *baroque,* a word use to describe a misshaped pearl!

Baroque architects expressed their faith by combining architecture, sculpture, painting, and other decorative arts. The result was both spiritual and dramatic. The elaborate decoration of the altar pointed to the importance of the sacrifice of the Mass. In addition, the place where God's word was preached and where the doctrines of the Church were explained was given a greater emphasis.

The focus of the baroque church was to admit more light and to emphasize unity. The spiritual goals of the Church—to restore confidence and to energize the faith of the people—were made visible in vibrant and dramatic ways.

New Expressions

The Romanesque, Gothic, and baroque styles were used and adapted by architects throughout the eighteenth and nineteenth centuries. But there were no remarkable innovations in church design until the twentieth century. Then amazing things began to happen!

First there was the discovery of new materials, such as reinforced concrete, steel, and other alloys. New technologies also played a part in what became a radical new architecture.

Along with these material developments, there came the growth of the liturgical movement in the Church. It stressed that the design of a church should clearly reflect the liturgical acts being celebrated. The guiding principle of modern church architecture is that attention should be focused on what is most important—the celebration of the Eucharist. For this reason the altar is central. It is the table of the eucharistic sacrifice and meal; it is the symbol of Christ. Therefore the altar is no longer attached to the back wall of the apse; it is placed in the front of the sanctuary.

Often modern churches are built in circular form to allow the community to gather around the altar. Still others reflect in their design the surrounding environment of mountains, for example, or desert or ocean.

Picture yourself in a part of the country that you love. What kind of church would fit into this environment? Describe it as fully as you can.

Modern, Air Force Academy Chapel, *Colorado*

The Story in Art

Religious art—painting, sculpture, stained glass, and mosaics—has always been a part of our Christian experience. Let's take a look at a few expressions of religious art here, but remember to do more exploring on your own.

Most early Church art took the form of sculpture and carving (in wood, stone, and marble) and mosaics. Actually the earliest image we have of Jesus, which depicts him as the Good Shepherd, was carved from bone! Gothic churches are known for the beautiful carvings of Christ and the saints that decorate their doors and facades (fronts). But the Gothic churches are best known for their exquisite stained-glass windows, which look almost like jewels set against black velvet.

The Renaissance The explosion of ideas in the Renaissance on the nature and beauty of the human being stimulated a new kind of art as well. Two artists stand out above all others: Michelangelo Buonarroti (1475–1564) and Leonardo da Vinci (1452–1519).

Michelangelo, although he was the painter of the Sistine Chapel, thought of himself first of all as a sculptor, and his religious pieces are overwhelmingly powerful. You have probably seen pictures of his *Pietà* in St. Peter's in Rome (see page 72). He carved this statue when he was only twenty-three years old. It is a marvel of skill and spiritual beauty. The word *pietà* is used to describe any scene showing Jesus being taken down from the cross and placed in Mary's arms. Not so well known is another *Pietà* that he carved when he was an old man. In it he shows an elderly man lifting Christ's body off the cross. The face of the man is Michelangelo's face—a self-portrait. It is a face full of grief and regret.

Da Vinci, like Michelangelo, was a genius in many fields. He was a painter, an architect, an inventor, and an engineer, among other things. He is probably best known as a painter, and his most famous religious work is the *Last Supper* (see page 73).

Some monks in Milan asked Leonardo to paint the picture on the wall of their refectory, or dining area. A wall painting is called a *fresco*, and it is extremely difficult to do. Wet plaster is spread on the wall,

Middle Ages, **Mary with Jesus,** *Cathedral of Amiens, France*

Renaissance, **Pietà,** *Michelangelo, Florence*

Renaissance, **detail from a sketch,** ***Last Supper,** Da Vinci*

and the artist must apply the paints quickly, before the plaster hardens. There is not much room for error in this kind of art! Leonardo experimented with painting on *dry* plaster—an even more difficult skill.

Leonardo's *Last Supper* is simple, touching, and masterful. Jesus and the Twelve are caught for all time by the artist at the moment when Jesus says, "One of you will betray me." Each figure is vividly human and unique.

The Baroque

Do you remember the characteristics of baroque architecture? Two of the words used to describe it were *vibrant* and *dramatic*. These same adjectives describe baroque painting and sculpture. Look at the marble sculpture of Saint Teresa of Ávila by Bernini. It is full of movement and drama—almost as if a wind were blowing. Compare it with the *Good Shepherd* from the third century or Michelangelo's *Pietà*, and you will see a great difference. Baroque painting shows the same tendencies. There is a great interplay of light and darkness, so much so that it looks as though the art is lit by stage lights. The gestures and garments are depicted in dramatic motion, too.

The Twentieth Century

Now let's leap ahead four centuries. Just as church architects used new materials and new technologies, so did the artists. Look at the picture of the head of Christ below. How is this art different from the art of the Renaissance and baroque periods?

Sacred art always expresses the spirituality of the age in which it is done. But no matter what the age, sacred art always has the power to lift our spirits to God—if we are open to it.

Imagine you are an artist in the year 2020. You are asked to design a piece for your parish church. What would you choose to do? Why?

Modern, **Head of Christ**, Roualt

Baroque, **The Ecstasy of St. Teresa**, Bernini, Rome

The Music of the Church

Christians have always sung about their faith. We have fragments of religious music going as far back as the third century, and a vast treasury of music has grown since then.

From the eighth to the eleventh centuries, a particular form of music developed that is unique to the Catholic Church. It is called *plainchant*. (*Chant* comes from the Latin word for "song.") Later, after it was regulated by the Church under Pope Gregory, it was called *Gregorian chant*.

Gregorian chant began and was developed in the monasteries of Europe. The monks wrote simple musical lines to be used in chanting the Liturgy of the Hours and, later, the Liturgy of the Mass. Originally the chant was sung without any musical accompaniment—just the human voice praising God. The chant was written on a four-line staff, not on the five-line staff we use today. In the beginning the notes were simply dots on the staff. That is why, even today, the notes look like marks made with a flat stylus or quill.

In the 1990s a recording of Gregorian chant made by Benedictine monks went to the top of the musical charts all over the world. The sound of chant was being rediscovered and delighted in by new generations. What do you think people find so appealing in this music that is eight hundred years old and sung in Latin?

Listen to Gregorian chant for a few minutes. Try to do this in an atmosphere that is quiet and reflective. Share your reactions to what you have heard.

182

The Liturgical Stage

Did you know that much of modern drama has its roots in the Church? In the tenth century the monks composed music to accompany an explanation of the liturgy, especially for the great Church feasts. Then they also began to act out the stories. Here's an example.

The Easter gospel account tells of the visit of Mary Magdalene and the holy women to Christ's tomb. The monks wrote a commentary for it (called a *trope*). On Easter they sang the trope, and several members of the community acted out the characters in the story—the angel, Mary Magdalene, and the other women. Later the drama was extended to include the story of Peter and John at the tomb. The earliest surviving copy of the play (from about 975) also included some stage directions and ideas for costumes: The apostles were to wear red vestments, and Peter was to limp badly!

The final addition to this play was the garden scene, in which Christ appears to Mary and she thinks at first that he is the gardener. The stage directions called for Christ to be in a white garment stained with blood. He was to carry a cross through the monastery apse before appearing to Mary. Afterward he was to return holding the resurrection banner.

As time passed, new forms of religious drama appeared. Unlike the monastic dramas, these were written and performed by laypeople. Also unlike the liturgical dramas, these were performed in the language of the people and placed much more emphasis on spectacle and entertainment.

A distinct kind of religious drama called a miracle play developed in the twelfth century. A *miracle play* is a dramatization of a saint's life with special emphasis on the saint's miracles. The stories were drawn from legendary accounts of popular saints combined with a healthy dose of imagination! This kind of religious drama became extremely popular throughout Europe.

As the plays began to include more spectacle and even comedy, their performance was removed from the church to the square outside. A modern

Passion play, San Antonio, Texas

development of a miracle play is the passion play of Oberammergau, Germany. It is presented every ten years in gratitude for the town being saved from a plague in 1632.

Still later in the Middle Ages came a third kind of religious drama called a morality play. A *morality play* is a drama in which virtues and vices are personified. This means that they are portrayed as people who speak and act.

The basic theme of a morality play is a conflict between the forces of good (the angels, the virtues) and the forces of evil (the devil, the vices). For example, the morality play *Magnificence* tells the story of a ruler who is deceived by false men (vices) and ruined by them. He is left to the mercy of Adversity and Poverty and eventually falls into the clutches of Despair. But he is rescued by Hope and is restored to power and grace.

Morality plays were very popular and continued to be performed well into the sixteenth century.

Can you think of a saint whose life would be a good subject for a miracle play? Describe the story.

things to think about

True art has the power to move us, to stir our imagination, to lift our spirit. Is there something unique and different about sacred art? What is it?

things to share

Imagine that you have been asked to write a modern morality play. How would you show the conflict between good and evil in today's world? What vices and virtues would you personify? Why?

WORDS TO REMEMBER

Find and define the following:

flying buttresses _____
_____
_____

Gregorian chant _____
_____
_____

OnLine
WITH THE PARISH

Modern forms of miracle plays are presented in many parishes—a Christmas play, for example. In some parishes young people come together during Lent to enact a "living" stations of the cross. You may wish to initiate or participate in one of these religious dramas in your parish.

Life in the Spirit

Gather in a circle. Bring with you any project or activity you have worked on for this chapter. Listen quietly to the sound of the chant.

Leader: Loving God of all creation, we place before you the work of our hands and the desires of our hearts. May these prosper and succeed. And may all that we are and all that we do always give glory to your name.

All: Amen, Alleluia!

Architects: Father, help us to use our gifts to raise hearts and minds to you.

All: Prosper the work of our hands!
Prosper the work of our hands!

Artists: Jesus, may our lives be our greatest works of art. Help us to discover—and to uncover—your image in us and in others.

All: Prosper the work of our hands!
Prosper the work of our hands!

Musicians: Holy Spirit, sing through us a constant song of praise and joy so that others may hear and join their voices to ours in prayer.

All: Prosper the work of our hands!
Prosper the work of our hands!

Actors: Loving God of all creation, use our voices, our bodies, and our emotions to tell the story of your love. Help us to express your word in all we do.

All: Prosper the work of our hands!
Prosper the work of our hands!

Hymn: Joyful, joyful we adore thee,
God of glory, Lord of love;
Hearts unfold like flowers before thee,
Praising thee, their Sun above.
Melt the clouds of sin and sadness,
Drive the dark of doubt away;
Giver of immortal gladness,
Fill us with the light of day.

All: May the favor of the Lord
our God be ours.
Prosper the work of our hands!
Prosper the work of our hands!

PRAISE BE TO YOU,
O LORD AND FATHER.

Praise be to you and you alone.
We praise you, O Lord, for all of your
  creatures,
Especially Brother Sun.
For Brother Sun, he is strong and bright,
And he gives us light as we live each day.

Praise also Sister Moon
And the sparkling stars
Which thy Hand made.

Praise thee, O Lord, for our Brother
  the Wind,
For weather that's cloudy and weather
  that's clear.
Praise thee, O Lord, for sweet Sister Water,
Helpful to all thy children here.

Praise thee, O Lord, for our Brother Fire.
Praise how he warms and lights the night.
Praise thee, O Lord, for the Earth our
  Mother,
She who sustains us that we might
Be led to a love of all creatures great
  and small
As they show thy grace.

Lord, help us each to learn.
Everywhere we turn
We can see thy Face.

Praise thee, O Lord, for all those who suffer
Injuries in thy Holy Name.
Blessed are they who merit to suffer.
You will reward them for their pains.

Praise be to you, O Lord of all seasons.
Praise be to you, O Lord, for all reasons.

Glory to you, O God!
Glory to you, O God!
Glory to you, O God, and you alone!

Saint Francis of Assisi

PARAPHRASE OF THE CANTICLE
OF BROTHER SUN

WE BEG YOU, LORD,
TO HELP AND DEFEND US.

Deliver the oppressed.
Pity the insignificant.
Raise the fallen.
Show yourself to the needy.
Heal the sick.
Bring back those of your people
  who have gone astray.
Feed the hungry.
Lift up the weak.
Take off the prisoners' chains.

May every nation come to know
that you alone are God,
that Jesus is your Child,
that we are your people, the sheep
  that you pasture. Amen.

Saint Clement of Rome

PRAYER FOR ALL NEEDS

I KNOW THAT
AT TIMES I WILL BE TROUBLED,

I know that at times I will be belaboured,
I know that at times I will be disquieted,
but I believe that I will not be overcome.
Amen.

Julian of Norwich

WORDS OF COMFORT

THE BREAD WHICH
YOU DO NOT USE

Is the bread of the hungry.
The garment hanging in your wardrobe
   Is the garment of one who is naked.
The shoes that you do not wear
   Are the shoes of one who is barefoot.
The money you keep locked away
   Is the money of the poor.
The acts of charity you do not perform
   Are so many injustices you commit.

Saint Basil the Great
A MEDITATION

LET NOTHING
DISTURB YOU,

nothing cause you fear;
All things pass
God is unchanging.
Patience obtains all:
Whoever has God
Needs nothing else,
God alone suffices.

Saint Teresa of Ávila
REFLECTION ON PATIENCE

O LORD, SUPPORT US
ALL THE DAY LONG,

until the shadows lengthen,
and the evening comes,
and the busy world is hushed,
and the fever of life is over,
and our work is done.
Then in your mercy,
grant us a safe lodging,
and a holy rest,
and peace at the last.

John Henry Newman
A NOVEMBER PRAYER

AGAIN WE KEEP
THIS SOLEMN FAST,

A gift of faith from ages past,
This Lent which binds us lovingly
To faith and hope and charity.

More sparing, therefore, let us make
The words we speak, the food we take,
Our sleep, our laughter, ev'ry sense;
Learn peace through holy penitence.

Saint Gregory the Great
A LENTEN PRAYER

JESUS,
I FEEL WITHIN ME

a great desire to please you
but, at the same time,
I feel totally incapable of doing this
without your special light and help,
which I can expect only from you.

Accomplish your will within me—
even in spite of me.

Saint Claude La Colombière SJ
PRAYER FOR LIGHT AND HELP

LORD, I BELIEVE
IN YOU: INCREASE MY FAITH.

I trust in you: strengthen my trust.
I love you: let me love you more and more.
I am sorry for my sins: deepen my sorrow.

I worship you as my first beginning,
I long for you as my last end,
I praise you as my constant helper,
and call on you as my loving protector.

Guide me by your wisdom,
correct me with your justice,
comfort me with your mercy,
protect me with your power.

Attributed to Pope Clement XI
SELECTIONS FROM THE UNIVERSAL PRAYER

HOW HOLY
THIS FEAST

in which Christ is our food:
his passion is recalled,
grace fills our hearts,
and we receive a pledge of the
   glory to come.

Saint Thomas Aquinas
A COMMUNION PRAYER

GLORY BE TO GOD
THE FATHER,

Praise to his coequal Son,
Adoration to the Spirit,
Bond of love, in Godhead one!
Blest be God by all creation
Joyously while ages run!

Saint Thomas Aquinas
PRAYER OF PRAISE

O MY GOD,
I DESIRE TO LOVE YOU

and to make you loved.
I desire to accomplish your will perfectly.
I desire, in a word, to be a saint.
But I feel my helplessness
and I beg you, O my God,
to be yourself my sanctity.

Saint Thérèse of Lisieux
PRAYER OF LOVE

REMEMBER,
O MOST LOVING VIRGIN MARY,

that never was it known that anyone who
fled to your protection, implored your help,
or sought your intercession was left
unaided. Inspired by this confidence,
we fly unto you, O virgin of virgins, our
mother. To you we come, before you we
stand, sinful and sorrowful. O mother
of the Word incarnate, despise not our
petitions, but in your mercy hear and
answer me.

Saint Bernard
THE MEMORARE

PRAYERS

LORD OF THE HARVEST,

YOUR WORD FINDS A HOME IN OUR HEARTS,

calls us into community and invites us to generous service of the human family. Bless with courage and spirit your priestly people, called to full participation in the one body of Christ. May many choose to respond in public service to your call offered in Jesus' name. Amen.

Joseph Cardinal Bernardin
PRAYER FOR VOCATIONS

I ARISE TODAY

THROUGH GOD'S STRENGTH TO PILOT ME,

God's might to uphold me,
God's wisdom to guide me,
God's eye to look before me,
God's ear to hear me,
God's hand to guard me,
God's way to lie before me,
God's shield to protect me,
God's host to save me from the
    snare of the devil.

A PRAYER OF SAINT PATRICK

LORD,

TEACH ME TO BE GENEROUS.

Teach me to serve you as you deserve.
Grant me, O Lord, to give to you and not
    to count the cost;
To fight for you and not to mind the
    wounds;
To toil and not to seek for rest;
To labor, but to ask for no reward except
    the knowledge
    that I do it for you, O Lord.

Saint Ignatius Loyola
TEACH ME, LORD

LORD JESUS,

YOU CHOSE TO BE CALLED

the friend of sinners.
By your saving death and resurrection
free me from my sins.
May your peace take root in my heart
and bring forth a harvest
of love, holiness, and truth.

A PRAYER FOR FORGIVENESS

Index